TRIGGER WARNINGS

TRIGGER WARNINGS

EDITED BY

JOAN HAWKINS AND
KALYNN HUFFMAN BROWER

CEPHALOPOD PRESS

CEPHALOPOD PRESS

Salish Sea, International Waters

First Edition: 1 3 5 7 5 6 4 2 8 8 8 8 8 8 8 8

ISBN: 979-8-88596-193-6
LOC: 2023915925

Design and Layout: Tony Brewer
Edits: Paul "The Psychic Octopus" Schreiber
Interior and Cover Photos: Anya Royce Peterson, PhD

Cover photo: Bealanabrack River at Maam, Ireland. 2015.
Frontis: Big Sur, California. 2008.
Part One: Promenade, Budapest, Hungary. 2014.
Part Two: Faery Tree in the Burren, Co. Clare, Ireland. 2008.
Part Three: Heart Tree, Bloomington. 2020.
Part Four: Grasses in the Burren, Ireland. 2014.
Part Five: Single gazania bloom, Berkeley Marina. 2010.
Author Bios: Alice's zinnias, Bloomington Farmers' Market. 2008.
Anya: Rip tide, South Beach, Point Reyes, California. 2011

CONTENTS

INTRODUCTION

WE BEGAN THIS VOLUME IN 2017, SHORTLY AFTER DONALD Trump was elected. We began working on it in response to the outrage we felt over the Access Hollywood Tape, in which Trump openly admitted that he randomly assaulted women. While previous presidential candidates' campaigns had been derailed when sex scandals were reported by the press (Gary Hart, for example), Trump seemingly faced no consequences, even when multiple accusations of physical molestation and rape were made against him. His election and imperviousness to charges of assault seemed to signal a new step in the normalization of rape culture. That while lamentable, sexual harassment and assault didn't really matter in the political arena. Or at least had no public service consequences for perpetrators.

It was in this climate that we began soliciting stories, poems, essays and nonfiction pieces about the assault and attempted assault that is a striking aspect of so many women's psychosexual histories. The original working title of the book was "Rape Escapes" because the pieces we solicited focused on deflection, escape and survival. We renamed the volume "Trigger Warnings" to set a different tone and to reflect the fact that so many of the pieces—workshopped and developed in public readings—required trigger warnings to the audience.

As we worked on the book, sexual harassment, rape, and the brutalization of women continued to serially dominate the news cycle. Even though Trump himself remained immune to prosecution, other powerful men—many in the media industry—were fired or resigned in the face of the newly emergent #MeToo Movement's revelations. Every time we sponsored public readings of contributions to this volume, audience members would approach us to say that they, too, had a story, and ask if we were we still accepting submissions.

We were also asked why we felt the need to tell such painful stories. "Because of Maya Angelou," we invariably said. Angelou was raped when quite young and lost the ability to speak for 5 years. When she finally recovered her voice, she found she had a lot to say. Her wonderful autobiography, *I Know Why the Caged Bird Sings*, is banned in many schools because of its frank and graphic depiction of rape. People frequently asked Angelou why she'd felt the need to describe the assault in such detail. Her response comes very close to our purpose in compiling this volume. She habitually said that she wanted people to understand the complexities of rape, and that she hoped any rape survivor reading her work would be able to move beyond blaming herself, open her own cage, and fly free. We hold the same wish for our readers, and recommend they read *I Know Why the Caged Bird Sings* as a companion volume.

All but one of the pieces in this anthology were authored by writers who belong to The Writers Guild at Bloomington, a nonprofit organization dedicated to promoting written and spoken word in Bloomington, Indiana and its environs. Most of us are published writers and all of us have other careers. Ruth Novaczek, the author of the Introductory piece in the book, is a London-based filmmaker and artist. We contacted her when she posted an earlier version of this story on her Facebook page. It was such a strong piece, we thought it would be perfect as a kind of thematic introduction. "Rape-escapes," she wrote when she sent us permission to use her story, "are a good way to show that every young woman has probably had one, and we're the lucky ones."

The anthology includes:

"Posted on Facebook" by Ruth Novaczek

Novaczek shares the time she and a friend escaped their would-be rapists through a backdoor of a bar.

Part One
"Variation on the Theme of Rape Escape" by Bronislava Volková

In this stream of conscious prose poem, Volková shares her layered experience of rape.

"Philosophy Lessons" by Joan Hawkins

Hawkins tells the story of the night her best friend was raped by their philosophy professor, the devastating effect on her bright, young friend, and the grief of a survivor, amazed she didn't recognize the trap.

"Fifteen" by Cara Hohlt

Hohlt tells the details of a night when she called a friend to comfort her through a broken heart. But his idea of providing comfort is to rape her before she realizes what's happening.

"Get Away" by Shana Ritter

Ritter remembers hitchhiking through Europe as young student and the time she fled through the woods to escape a man who intended to rape and then kill her.

Part Two
"The Park" by Antonia Matthews

Matthews remembers a lovely, joyful park with a view of the Welsh mountains, where a friendly man chews on a stalk of warm grass and coaxes her to sit and wait with him.

Two poems by Hiromi Yoshida

"NYC Chinatown" evokes the visceral feelings, taste, textures, impatience, curiosity, and the inner voice that drives little girls to run away from a vulgar stranger.

"IN v. LDS" contemplates the bruised mouths and sunken breasts, the shame and truncated justice of rape.

Two memoir shorts by Darlene Jolly

"It Was the Summer of 1956" remembers a near rape event when as a young girl, teenage boys on bicycles surround the author.

In "The Cave" Jolly tells her path of healing from childhood sexual abuse.

Two poems and an essay by Hílda Davis

"The Cure" dives into the physically painful aftermath of rape.

"Plan B May Not Work" recounts the double trauma of a violent encounter with a violent man and the judgement she faces when seeking to terminate the pregnancy.

"On Hunger and Facing Something Terrible" Davis unpacks the consequences of repressing the memory of a college party date rape.

Part Three

"Escaping Beaver Trapper" by Kalynn Huffman Brower

Brower tells the story of how she escaped from Beaver Trapper, a hippie cowboy truckdriver who wanted to take her home to his sculpture studio.

"La Fatale" by James Dorr

Le Vampire, a woman with forbidden cravings, finds she can best be sated by using her sharp nails and teeth to protect her innocent friends.

"Caramel" by Tom Bitters

A gang of miners assault a teenage girl who works in a Rocky Mountain brothel.

"Strange Fire" by Caroline Geduld

A married woman has a brief sexual encounter with a stranger and, now consumed by the fire of desire, stalks a younger man.

Part Four
"Between a Rock and a Dream Job" by Janet Cheatham Bell
Bell recounts the story of her dream job as book editor, when she faces the twin insults of racism and sexism and stands up to a sales rep who pimps for her publishing company president.

"I Want to Go Home. Now!" by Maria Hamilton Abegunde
Abugunde's essay contemplates her gift of clairvoyance and a time she foresaw danger and escaped a rapist.

Part Five
"Persephone" a lyrical poem by Zilia Balkansky-Sellés
Balkansky-Sellés contemplates the rape of Persephone, connecting her ancient loss to the current ravages upon our once fruitful planet, Earth.

We would like to thank the Writers Guild at Bloomington for its support of the project, and the audiences who made suggestions and offered help. Anya Royce contributed the lovely photographs that separate sections of the book. Marty Belcher, Kyle Quass and Urban Deer supported us with music at public readings. Tony Brewer designed and produced the book. And, of course, we owe a great debt of gratitude to the spouses, family, lovers and friends who provided love, encouragement, and coffee along the way.

Joan Hawkins & Kalynn Huffman Brower, 2023

TRIGGER WARNINGS

POSTED ON FACEBOOK

RUTH NOVACZEK

I WAS IN ITALY, TRAVELING AROUND TUSCANY WITH A FRIEND.
We arrived in the evening at a small village, the atmosphere was weird, we didn't know was fascist, we ate in a restaurant and asked if there was somewhere to stay. Two guys at another table said they were going to the next village and offered us a lift.

We got in the car, and I pretended I couldn't speak Italian, I listened to what they were saying, they were planning to rape us, so I suggested in terrible Italian, that we stop at a bar for a drink.

We found a place by the roadside and went inside, I walked up to a large family sitting at the back and told them these guys wanted to rape us. They said, well you American putanas, coming here, we're decent people. . . I told my friend we should go to the bathroom together and find a way out, I dragged my friend out the back door,

Behind the bar was a wood, quite dense pines, we ran and ran, we somehow found a monastery, we rapped on the door. They didn't ask us questions, and showed us to a dormitory full of virgin Mary statuary, we woke up early and in the morning and left. . . that's all I can remember, we escaped.

My friend was angry because she said I'd been bossy and didn't talk to me for the rest of the day, I said "they were going to rape us and you didn't understand."

Our friendship never recovered

PART ONE

VARIATION ON THE THEME OF RAPE ESCAPE

(STREAM OF CONSCIOUSNESS)

BRONISLAVA VOLKOVÁ

I AM HAPPY. MEN ABHOR ME. I CAN'T STAND THEM THEY ARE vicious. They are obnoxious, they make me sick. I can't even look at them. I do not want to see them. Men are evil. They make me puke. They are disgusting, cold, unforgivable, bland, hateful. They are dead. I don't want to hear their voices. Their bodies can be beautiful, but only when they are not real. When they act like the wild primitive tribal men. After that, they are dirty. They are selfish. They are deaf. They don't belong here. They are pitiful. They are dead. They need to be dead. They have died. I killed them. I killed them. They deserve to die. They are dead. I choked them to death. They have no life left in them. I am hot. I burn. I fly. I am an angel in heaven. I am not coming back. They make me nauseous. I want to close my eyes. I will not see them again. Never again. They will not hurt me again. They can't. They are pitiful. I am not here. I am gone. They are only shadows. All of them are shadows. They never make it to be real. It doesn't hurt, because they are only shadows. I live. I am gone. I see everything. It doesn't frighten me. I am gone. They can't reach me. I am safe. I am spirit. They can't touch me. They no longer have power over me. I am gone. Rape is just a ridiculous act, which doesn't exist. There is no pain. My father's penis is disgusting. Why do they have them? It seems so ridiculous! I don't need them. I certainly don't like them. I will not talk to them. I am free. Why did I think I needed to talk to them? Because they were there? But they are not here. They seem to be every-where. But I am invisible. They cannot touch me. I shall no longer talk to them. You can't appease a devil. Let them eat their own flesh. That's it! Let them eat their own flesh! I am gone. One more vibration and I am gone entirely, out of reach. I am in heaven. Now they can't get to me. I am a spirit coming back to heal, but not by letting them touch me. That was the mistake. Not by letting them touch me. I hate them for touching me. For they cannot touch: they left their spirit at home. They will hear the bells ring, then they will heal. I will force them to heal. I will force them to hear. I will be given the gift of sound. I sound. I, sound. I am. God bless my role in the plan of salvation.

PHILOSOPHY LESSONS

JOAN HAWKINS

THE NIGHT PAUL THURMAN RAPED MY BEST FRIEND, HE GAVE me a ride home. Or—to be more precise—he gave me a ride to my mother's. It was so late the electric trolley cars had stopped running. So my plan was to walk to my mom's apartment—a few blocks away—and spend the night there. Paul thought I was crazy. "You can stay here," he said. "Sleep on the couch." But I wanted to leave. You see, Paul—*Dr. Thurman*—was the chair of the philosophy department at the State College I attended. And the thought of waking up on his couch—No toothbrush. Funky clothes. The social obligation to make small talk over morning coffee—was mortifying. The evening had been strange enough; morning would be downright freaky.

I'd come with a group of philosophy students who'd worked all evening compiling the department's fall course descriptions. Holed up in Dr. Thurman's office—typing, mimeographing, collating, stapling—we'd been told he wouldn't be there. And early in the evening, it looked like he would leave. But then he didn't and, at the end of the work session, he offered us drinks and pizza at his place. A way of saying thank you, he said. So we piled into a couple of VW buses and drove out to the Sunset District. There were about 6 of us. Meredith, me, and 4 graduate students—all men.

At Thurman's, the wine and vodka flowed free, the drinks were very strong, and that pizza we were supposed to be ordering never quite got dialed in. Meredith got into an argument with some graduate student over Heidegger. The grad student was defending him and Meredith was livid. "He was a fucking Nazi," she kept saying. In another corner, another grad student—this one with a tiny goatee and a passion for Kant, was holding forth on the Sublime. I retreated to the hearth, poking the ashes and feeding the fire. I tried taking a few small sips from my drink to keep it from spilling over. But even those were too strong, so I set the glass aside and waited for Meredith to finish her quarrel, so we could leave. All the while Paul Thurman stayed in the background. Once he'd written a brilliant essay about the pre-Socratic notion of constancy applied to the odds of winning in Vegas. And now, leaning against the bookcase, he watched, and waited to see which way the chips and the ladies would fall.

As I said, we—Meredith and me—were the only two ladies present. And looking back now, I'm amazed I didn't recognize the trap. No food, strong drinks, hot apartment. And then that moment when Paul peeled himself loose from the bookcase, took Meredith and me by the elbow, and led us out to see his midnight garden. When we came back inside, the grad students had left. That's when I called my mother. Who offered to pick us up. I wanted to walk and I thought the air would help us both—Meredith and me.

But that last drink had hit Meredith hard. By the time I came back to the living room, she was stretched out on the sofa, the room spinning around her. And she had already accepted Paul's invitation to spend the night. "Are you sure?" I asked, just often enough to annoy her. "You can come with me. My mom won't mind." "Positive," she said.

By the time I started collecting my things, she was already asleep— or perhaps passed out, the firelight flickering across her face, casting gothic shadows. A burnt out cigarette stub still in her hand. Thinking about the hangover she was sure to have, I tried one last time to wake her. But she was out cold, and only shivered a little when I shook her shoulder. I remember Paul looking very fatherly, as he told me it was better for her to stay there. "She's too drunk to walk," he said. "And I don't think I can carry her. It's *all right*. She's stayed here before. Other students have stayed here."

Whistling a little, he went in the hall and came back with a pastel armful of blankets. Together, we covered Meredith with a small pink and green quilt. Meredith was taller than me, but she looked tiny under the blanket. And I wondered why she'd never told me that she and Thurman were friends. "We weren't," she told me later. "We aren't."

As for him—he'd always been so derisive of the Marxist students. Hard to imagine philosophy sleepovers at his place. Feminists talking dialectical materialism with the Dept Chair until the last street car had gone. But then, perhaps his wife would have taken an interest. He used to have a wife.

"Are you sure you don't want to stay?" Paul asked me. "I have plenty of blankets."

"Positive," I answered.

"At least finish your drink," he said, holding out the glass I'd abandoned earlier.

"No, thanks," I said, shaking my head. What I wanted at the moment was some fresh air, some food, and a cup of my mother's hot cocoa. I knew she'd be waiting up for me, curious to know why I hadn't gone home.

"Well let me give you a ride," Paul said. "The neighborhood isn't safe."

We didn't talk much in the car. "Chilly night." "Big day tomorrow." A volley of little phrases. Just enough to take the edge off the silence. When we got to my mom's, Paul double parked and waited. But when I opened the car door, he leaned over, grabbed my arm and said, "I just want you to know, I wish you'd been the one who stayed."

Then with a little shove, he pushed me out and drove off. Leaving me standing in the street thinking of every weird creepy thing he'd ever said. That beginning of the term party I didn't attend. Meredith told me later he'd asked about me and seemed disappointed when she told him I'd gone to visit my boyfriend. "Oh," he'd reportedly said, "she has a boyfriend." And that time Meredith and I stood in the hallway, asking Dr. Silverman if we could write a collaborative paper. "Hey Jim," Paul—Dr. Thurman—called as he walked past, two of his own students in tow.

"How come you get the pretty ones?" And tonight, when he stood behind my chair as I typed his course description, and leaning just a little too close, he asked about the perfume I was wearing. "It suits you," he'd said. "Sweet with a lot of spice." And the fact that he was willing to give me a ride to my mother's, but hadn't offered to drive me and Meredith home. Or even to West Portal, where we could have gotten a bus.

My ankle hurt—maybe I'd twisted it when he pushed me out of the car, and I limped as I walked toward the sidewalk. When I got to the curb, I vomited.

My mother didn't think Meredith was in any danger. In her world, bosses didn't have to physically force themselves on women. It was the truck drivers and your fellow workers—with their sidelong glances, sweaty muscled arms and quick hands that you had to be careful of. Bosses just called you into the office—cut your hours, split your shift, moved you to a team where the work was harder and more dangerous— unless. . . Mom had frequently changed jobs because of her bosses. But she had never had to fight one off with a dispatch rack. "He's the Chair of the Philosophy Department," she told me now. "He's not going to rape a girl who's passed out on his couch. And it doesn't sound like he's inter- ested in her. But you'd be better careful because you could find yourself in a bad situation."

It was the one time I listened to my mother and wish I hadn't.

The one time Mom was wrong.

I didn't see Meredith in class the following morning. But she did meet me for lunch at the Mexican Restaurant where we always ate. Big enchilada platters and a salad for $3. Free coke. And mangoes when they were in season. Perfect for construction workers and impoverished students.

Meredith was sitting at a corner table, away from the windows. She was wearing a black turtleneck sweater and jeans, clothes I had never seen her wear before. No jewelry, no makeup. Very pale, with only her dark hair and sweater standing out against the white and blue walls. She ordered a bowl of soup, which she didn't eat, and a cup of black coffee. When she turned her head I noticed that her lip was swollen and her cheek was bruised.

"What happened?" I asked, whispery as though we were sharing secrets in class.

She woke up after Paul came back, she told me. She didn't know what time it was. Just that when she woke up, he was inside her. He smelled awful, she said. "Like that weird sick smell you get with a fever." After he climaxed he got up, handed her a tissue, and went into the bedroom. She waited. Maybe 20 minutes, she guessed, because she heard the entire first side of *Rubber Soul* playing through the wall. When the apartment was finally quiet, she got dressed and walked home. She was still bleeding.

Pointing to my own cheek, I asked if he had hit her. "No," she said. She had fallen on the way home. A couple of times. And no, she did *not* want to go to the clinic. And she did NOT want to file a police report. "Are you kidding?" she said. "He's the Chair of the Philosophy Department. I'm a hippie chick, with an active sex life, and I was drunk. They'd rake me over the fucking coals."

I didn't ask about filing a complaint with the school. There was no institutional way to file such a complaint back then. No disciplinary action that could be taken, as far as any of us knew. Women who had bad experiences wrote abbreviated tales on the bathroom walls, warning others. I imagined Meredith would leave such a warning about Paul. In her signature green ink, letters tilting a little to the right. "If Thurman invites you to his place—don't go—" she'd write, "even with friends. Speaking from experience."

A week later she left school. "Where's Meredith?" Dr. Silverman asked me. "Is she ill?"

"Yes," I said, thinking of Aristotle's sickness of the soul. "I don't know when she'll be back."

It was a year before I saw Meredith again. I was married by then and living in Santa Cruz. She was moving from Los Angeles to Ukiah, and she stopped to spend the night. She was bright and jittery, all jangling bangle bracelets and beads, full of stories and plans that didn't quite make sense. My brother came by to deliver some chairs and stayed for dinner. We spent a mad evening. Meredith drinking brandy and telling my ultra-conservative brother that she wanted to go work with the

Tupamaro Guerillas in Uruguay. He thought she meant gorillas, and kept asking "like Jane Goodall? I thought you studied philosophy." Laughing and never answering his question, Meredith kept repeating "Tupamaro guerillas" in syncopated time as she reached for the brandy bottle.

She passed out that night, too. My husband carried her to the sofa, and we tried to make her comfortable with a pillow and a small blue quilt. Looking down at her, I shivered as the memory of that awful night reached out its withered hand.

She cut out early the next morning before anyone else was up. Left an effusive thank you note on the kitchen table. She'd made coffee, she said, and nabbed a bagel. She'd call when she got settled.

I never heard from her again. I tried contacting her parents, but they'd moved—and there were thousands of Brennans. In recent years, I've tried searching for her online—Google, Facebook, Instagram. I even tried one of those "we can find anyone" services. No luck. And so we have never had that conversation—

"You left me there."

"You wouldn't come with me."

The conversation I thought might mend our friendship.

About 10 years after Meredith was raped, I saw Dr. Jim Silverman at a reading. He told me Meredith's father had called him. Had said Meredith was "disturbed," and a "pathological liar." And he wanted Jim's help in having her involuntarily committed. Jim had refused.

A few days later, I ran into Paul Thurman at Top Dog, Berkeley's anarcho-libertarian sausage place. Cramped and greasy, with newspaper clippings, Emma Goldman quotes and poetry scotch taped to the walls, it was an odd place to encounter a pre-Socratic Philosophy Don and rapist. He was seated at the counter, with his back to the door—so I didn't notice him at first and he did not see me. But when I gave the barman my order, he—this leather-jacketed man at the counter—sat up very straight and turned. Paul Thurman. A little heavier, a little older, shorter hair. But definitely Paul Thurman. "I'd know that voice anywhere," he said, extending his hand. Warm high school reunion smile, just like we were two old friends bumping into each other after a lifetime spent apart.

In my mind's eye, I saw Meredith. Sitting cross-legged on her living room floor, shuffling Tarot cards, fanning them out, selecting three. Afterwards, she threw the I Ching. "I'm leaving," she told me.

What do you say to the man who ruined your friend's life? The man who had wanted to ruin yours?

At Top Dog, an ancient black and white TV set, perched precariously over the grill, played noon-time reruns of the old *Perry Mason* show. I told Jake the grill master that I wanted my order to go. Cutting narrowed eyes at Paul, he nodded. I was one of his best customers and he didn't know this man from Adam. But he'd picked up the vibe. "Some jerk driving our regulars away," I could hear him telling his partner. And I had a feeling I'd get a free coffee next time around.

I paid for my sausage and my drink, got some Russian mustard from the bar, onions, peppers, napkins—all the while Paul sitting there, looking at me, silence spreading out between us. What do you say to the man who ruined your friend's life? The man who had wanted to ruin yours.

"I loved that show as a kid," I finally said, jerking my head toward the T.V. "Assholes always confessed, and they always paid. Too bad life isn't like that."

Passive-aggressive, I know. But direct confrontation would have meant saying Meredith's name. Hearing excuses and denials and " I thought she wanted to; I thought that's why she stayed." Or even worse, "I don't remember." Listening to *his* side of the story. And I couldn't bear that.

By this time Jake and the two other people at the counter were staring at us. I stuffed some money in the tip jar, nodded to Jake, and walked out.

What do you say to the man who ruined your friend's life? Not much, as it turns out. You just tell her story and say a few cryptic words to your fellow travelers at the bar.

FIFTEEN

CARA HOHLT

THAT RING CAME BACK TO HER, AFTER IT HAPPENED, THE ring that the wrong guy gave her.

But it all started with the right guy. She stood with her boyfriend, foreheads together, his eyes so green when he dared to look at her between his words. His parents had found out again. Sadie already knew, really, when Jason showed up at her front door. The way he held himself, only took a few steps inside. But here it was again, like last year in the orchestra closet when they broke up the first time, or the second, when they talked on the stairs behind the stage curtains. She'd hold on this time.

She ran her fingers through his hair. Sometimes it smelled like the wooden floors backstage, or like the caramel that they dipped cones into at DQ when they were working. She asked why. He said it was the girl from church that told on them, the one from orchestra class who'd seen them the night before. Shouldn't have gone out together alone, he said. She agreed. But she'd wanted to, so much, just the two of them. She liked hanging out with Brooke and Matt too, of course. Brooke was her best friend. And Matt was—

Jason reached his hands to his head, took hold of her fingers there. One more kiss, please, she thought. Then a tear fell from his cheek and dropped to the floor. He turned and pushed himself out the screen door, running.

The pain lit within. She couldn't cry. She stood alone, frozen, staring out the door. It was these moments, when she couldn't cry, that she'd

14

notice things small and intricate. Like the front steps. They were made of pebbles, and there were ants climbing the tiny rocks like a mountain range. Maybe he'd crushed some of them with his Converse sneakers as he ran. A long line of them traveled over the edge of the step and out of sight. Where did they go when they hurt? Should she go somewhere? The sun was too bright and she stayed fixed at the screen door, staring at ants and the last place she saw him.

The whole thing was stupid. Her eyes filled with tears and everything smeared into one messy laundry basket of images—her boyfriend running away, the summer flowers, the neighbors' cars, the sharp blue sky. Even the ants.

Damn! She kicked the metal plate on the screen door, denting it outward. Now her mom would know and scream at her. She kicked it again and turning, slammed her head into the doorframe three times. All she wanted was his sloppy brown hair in her fingers again. But instead, she took a rip at her own bangs.

Shoes came off her feet and flew across the room, just missing her mom's bedroom door. As if denting that could take back the mess she'd already made. Nobody gave a shit about her anyway. A door is more important. No one cared about clumps of her hair or the way he couldn't look at her when he let go of her hands. She slapped those hands against her face for being stupid enough to throw the shoes. You could have broken something else you dumb bitch.

She was going to get into so much trouble. She needed to call Brooke. Brooke, who was strong, who cared. Brooke, who even told Matt to stop being creepy, that it wasn't funny, that Jason was Sadie's boyfriend, not him. Brooke, who would always have Sadie over Saturday night so they could goof around Sunday morning, spying from the patio at Jason's family in the church parking lot as the crowd came and went. Brooke, who always had her back.

The phone was in Sadie's hand and it was begging to be slammed against the counter, the dial tone filling her head with too much noise. She punched the number pad instead, misdialed, hung up and tried again, one number at a time. She cradled the phone to her ear. She was pathetic, snot and tears running down her face like a stupid baby. Brooke would understand. She'd held Sadie's shoulders that time when Jason's parents parked their car right across from the patio and stared at the two of them as Jason got out of the back seat. He hadn't waved, and they all knew why. Fucking parents.

The phone was heavy, ringing too long. Why was it so wrong to fall in love with the boy you can't call, the boy who listens for your one ring so he knows you're at home, and if he's alone, calls you back? Why wouldn't anyone answer? She slammed the phone down on the counter-top, a sharp, loud smack jarring her thoughts. She inspected the plastic casing carefully for signs of damage. No cracks, she found, relieved. She held the thing to her ear, but it was silent. She put an index finger on the receiver and lifted it again. It hummed its boring drone.

Matt, then?

He'd probably be home by now. At least he'd be someone to talk to. The four of them had hung out all summer, bumming around town, watching the movies their parents wouldn't allow, talking about sex and trying pot at Matt's. And Matt was the guy who drove backwards past the drive-thru window at DQ, who told her dirty jokes in front of her manager, making Sadie blush. He said he liked her laugh.

There was the ring too. Matt had given it to her, a cheap knock-off wedding ring. It was a joke, of course. But she'd worn it for a little while anyway because it was pretty, and because Jason couldn't give her one. Brooke had told Matt it was creepy. Had told Sadie, too, and so Sadie gave it back to him. But Brooke wasn't here now, and wasn't answering the phone.

Sadie dialed Matt's number very slowly, her fingers very clumsy. When she heard his voice say hello, she choked up. He was full of con-cern. He told her hold on—he was on his way, right away he said. She told him the phone was ok, she just needed to talk, but he'd already hung up.

She slid to the floor and waited until his car pulled up to the curb. He took the steps fast. His face was there, through the screen. She wished it was Jason's. He made a comment about the dent as he came in. Yeah, I'm fucked, she said. It felt awkward, standing there together in the living room. He invited her to sit on her couch. They'd sat there before, the four of them, drinking her mom's Southern Comfort after school. His arm went around her shoulder. They were good friends, he said. She thought he meant the four of them, but then he said he hated to see her cry over that fucker who didn't stand up for her. He's not a fucker, she could never call her boyfriend that; it was just his parents, that's why they'd broken up again, that's all. It just hurt.

His arm squeezed her around the back. That's what a good friend does, doesn't he? He reached his free hand over to smear the tears on her cheek. His face got closer to hers. She felt kind of claustrophobic, as if a bit of sky were pushing into her lungs. The room seemed too bright with the sunlight pressing through the sheer curtains. His lips parted in a wet smile. His forehead bent to hers. She asked what he was doing. He didn't say anything. The fabric on the cushions caught her attention, each rough strand of fiber woven like a sweater. Everything went cream, the color of the couch, the color of her thighs at the edge of her shorts.

No. Even the carpet was cream. No, don't. There was only so much couch to scoot over, inch by inch. No, really. His arms were long and not very tan for all the time they spent horsing around this summer. Don't. The four of them. No. Four of them, doing donuts in the high school parking lot. No. Four of them, watching porn for the first time in Matt's basement. No. Four, getting ice cream from DQ. Four. Her boyfriend and her, Matt, Brooke. No. I don't want to. I don't. Don't. No.

Long arms and long legs wound around her from behind. The Berber carpet etched her knees like sandpaper on blocks of wood. The couch loomed on her right, as empty as her head. His hand appeared in front of her face, and on his pinkie finger was the ring, the cheap knock-off Brooke hated. His voice said something into the back of her hair like there you go. Long fingers wrapped themselves into the crevice of her shorts. The fingers moved up and down. They moved in the way a lawn mower moves in a neighbor's yard across the street. The shorts hiked up into her crotch. The carpet went all the way under the couch. Sheer curtains gleamed in the cold summer sun, for a few long moments while she made her decision. And as soon as possible, her shorts soaked through, warmly.

Just like that, he left. He said something about how hard she came. It didn't matter that she didn't hear him well. The screen door was still wide open, still dented. He smiled, saying he hoped she didn't catch hell from her mom. When his sneakers flew down the sidewalk to his car, she latched the lock. It was a tiny lock, midway up the screen, like the little switch in her crotch to click one way or the other. Then she shut the front door against the sunshine. She didn't hit or dent anything else. She saw the ring he left on the carpet, or perhaps she didn't, not yet. She just went to the phone and dialed Brooke's number again.

GET AWAY

SHANA RITTER

HE JERKED THE WHEEL SUDDENLY AND DROVE INTO THE PULL off. It was dark and there was nothing but trees looming even darker. His face was pallid in the dashboard light. A chill went up and down my whole body. It was microseconds. He began to reach, and in one fluid motion, I pulled a punch, grabbed my backpack, pulled up on the door handle, got out and ran for the woods. I couldn't see where I was going, I had no real idea where I was, but away from the car was much better than in the car or anywhere near it.

I heard him opening his door. His breath was audible behind me, and then it wasn't. There was the sound of leaves in the evening wind, the enveloping dark of the forest, a scent of wood and pine, the protection of the trees.

I always loved the woods, they were inviting, arms and nooks ready to offer me a quiet place. As a child I would find my way behind the cottage and enter well into their midst. There was a game I would play for hours, trying to move without making a sound, imagining someone pursuing me and my escape, never breaking a twig, never skittering a stone or acorn, stealth as an animal. Now it was real.

You knew it right away. You knew you should not take the ride. As soon as you opened the car door you felt that there was something strange about him. His close cropped hair, the heavy framed glasses, his fingers tight on the wheel of the Opel. It was a light blue sedan, it looked like every other car on the road. But you had been standing there awhile, a lot of cars had passed you by. It was starting to look like it could turn to rain. You wanted to make Hamburg before dark. You wanted to get through Germany as quickly as possible.

I knew I shouldn't have taken the ride. I knew it when my stomach rippled with a tightening and I got a sour taste in my mouth. There was a tingling in my hands. Warning. Warning. But even though every fiber of my body went into alert my rational mind told me something different. In a calm modulated male voice my head said, "Come on, it's such a good ride, you've been waiting here for over an hour, he's going your way, it'll be fine, you're overreacting."

I should know not to listen to my head over my gut. It's not like this was my first time hitchhiking on my own. When I was in high school I had often hitched rides into the city and back. After I graduated, I travelled across the U.S., around Israel, through England and Scotland. During college I often hitched from Buffalo back home to Rockland County. It added up to thousands and thousands of miles. Usually I hitched with a friend, or a traveling companion.

Used to be I'd hitch with my dog, a beautiful mixed German Shepherd. No one would stop who had any ill will with Rebel around. I wish he would have been with me this time.

It was the spring of 1976. I was travelling from Amsterdam to Copenhagen where I had friends and the possibility of some work. I stood by the side of the road on the outskirts of Amsterdam for a long time. I was used to getting rides pretty easily. It was unusual for me to be waiting. I never got in a car with just anyone. Usually, it was long hairs who stopped, young people like me who travelled often and liked meeting new people, sharing stories. We thought of ourselves as connected, a web of shared experiences that we were constantly adding to. And in that way, we would shift the way the world worked. We thought we were changing things for the better. Sometimes older women stopped out of a sense of protectiveness. That had happened a few times. Sometimes truckers wanting company on a long haul. Most often I met someone who would hitch hike with me but this time I was on my own. I hadn't worried much about it. This was Holland after all. The Dutch were generous and welcoming. Travelling through Germany may have made me a bit nervous but not the Netherlands.

The evenings were long this time of year, but it was creeping toward late afternoon and I wanted to be halfway to Copenhagen before dark. I wanted to be in Germany as short a time as possible. I am a first generation American who grew up with too many stories about Germany to feel safe there. I started getting worried I'd have to walk the mile or so to the last tram stop and then head back into the city and try and get a bed at the hostel.

Then a car pulled over. The guy was maybe late twenties, early thirties. Very clean cut. Short hair, black framed glasses. He didn't even try speaking to me in Dutch, went right into English, "Where are you going?" he asked. I was speaking to him through the window he'd lowered. As soon as my hand leaned on the door, I felt it. That twist in my stomach, that nervous energy in my body, that voice I didn't want to hear saying don't do it. I swallowed it. "I'm heading north, all the way to Copenhagen."

"Come on," he said "I'm going past Brennan, it will get you well on your way."

It was a good ride and he sounded ok, good English, no weird stuff in the car. I hesitated. I saw the clouds rolling in and felt the wind signal rain. Just go I said to myself, it'll be fine.

You started to lift the backpack that was at your feet. He said "well are you getting in or not? You shook your head, you meant to say no, but you opened the door and put the backpack at your feet and got in. He asked if you wanted to put your backpack in the back seat. "That's Ok," you said, "I'll just keep it here." He took off fast. And there you had your ride. Almost as far as you had planned to go. He put the radio on. He didn't try to make small talk. That was ok, but still you felt your shoulders tense and you kept a hold of your backpack. Let me know if you need to stop, he said but didn't glance your way. The city was left behind you.

While I felt better travelling with another woman, I'd met lots of really nice people. A Eurail pass was way beyond my means, and so not my style. The idea of travelling from place to place with a guidebook was not something that had ever occurred to me. I was a traveler, not a tourist. Travelers recognized each other by an exchange of looks, or by the way we looked. We worked our way around different languages, and even when we faulted words, we were able to carry on a conversation. There was a kind of code, an agreement, a connection. I knew this guy was not part of that, but I thought, it'll be ok.

I was alert but started to relax a bit. I kept my eyes on the road signs. We chatted just a little, the usual, where are you from, where are you going, but conversation was bumpy even as the highway rolled behind us and dusk started coming on. He grew quiet and I was just as glad not to be having to do much small talk. He put music on the radio, a kind of jazz without melody.

You drifted back to thinking of the last days in Amsterdam, so much music, so many people from all over. You had made it to the Van Gogh museum but never to Anne Frank's house, though you had read her book over and over as a girl. You had always been told that Holland was safe, kind and always been told to be wary of Germany. Your plan was to cross Germany as quickly as possible moving from the sanctuary of Anne Frank to the bravery of the Danish King. You attributed the wariness you were feeling to being in Germany. The car raced along, and a hint of a different language came over the radio.

As we went deeper into the forested landscape it seemed to get dark quickly. That's when I noticed his face changing. That's when I felt his tension, his hands gripping the wheel. The road changed. Taller, denser trees lined the meridian. It felt faster, narrower. There was nothing else around, no signs, no lights, no oncoming traffic that could be seen. Nothing. That's when he swerved into the turnoff, fast enough so I bounced against the door and then toward him. He grabbed in the direction of my throat. I thought he was saying something, but it was sounds, not words that came from him.

It was unexpected, but I was not surprised. That knot in my stomach had never gone away. So as he grabbed, I threw a punch that I didn't know I had in me. I threw the punch, grabbed he back and jumped out the door hightailing it into the woods all in one fluid moment. I was a deer under fire.

You had never hit anyone, but you knew what to do. Your hand became a fist, your arm a lever. Punch, open the door jump out run, run fast. You heard his car door opening, heard what you knew was a curse even though you didn't understand the words themselves, heard him coming in your direction then swear again. It was as if night was on your side because it got dark really quickly. You ran into the cover of the woods, and it felt like the woods you knew. The woods you used to hide in when you didn't want anyone in your family to find you. You knew how to move fast and then hold still and be quiet.

I really don't know where my strength came from, or my coordination, my fluidness of movement compared to his jerky angry grabs gave me some advantage, if you could call it that. I was sure if he caught me, he wasn't only going to rape me, he would kill me after. I saw it in that last glint of light in his narrowing eyes. I felt it in the muscles of his forearms and the claws of his fingers. I heard it in his rapid breathing, the tightening of his throat muscles, the hate I felt spewing from him as he reached over, as all his clenched up rage pounced at me.

It was so fast, and at the same time everything slowed way down, like a film in an old projector coming to a stop, click, click, click on each frame. I could see each muscle tightening, his Adam's apple like a piston, the lines around his eyes deepening, his nostrils flaring. I saw the nails on his fingers clean and short and shiny. Everything was aimed at me. Everything he had were weapons, points of fury. Nearly forty years later and I still see it in slow motion.

He had been so contained, so polite and soft spoken. But he grunted as he came at me and then he roared, then let out a sound like a cornered animal, as if he was the one about to be slaughtered. I ran right into that darkness. He stumbled after me for a few minutes. He screamed at me that he'd get me and then it turned to Dutch and cursing. I didn't hear anything and then I heard his hand slam against the car. It sounded closer than it was. I'd been running for what felt like twenty minutes but was likely only two. I crouched down then to catch my breath. I was well beyond any lights from the roadway. I was in the forest, the German forest, and while that could have held a horror for me it didn't. I was escaping from a man, a supposed gentle Dutch man who had turned into a monster, and it was only these woods that might save me.

I saw the beam from his flashlight then and I didn't dare move. He was still by the car and the light was distant, but I saw it, and I imagined him tracking me and getting closer and closer and I held my breath. Then the light went off and I heard the car doors slam, first the passenger side which I had left wide open and then the driver's side. I heard the engine race and I saw the lights from his car disappear. I stayed where I was maybe five minutes more, I had no watch, no flashlight, only matches, and I didn't dare to move. Not yet. I thought he might come back, I thought unrealistically that maybe he fooled me and didn't really drive off at all and he was waiting. I sat in the still dark leaning up against the tree.

I rose slowly and went further into the woods. Either the moon hadn't risen yet or it was a thin new crescent, or it was blocked by the trees. I was walking away from the road. I began to hear the forest's own noises around me. The branches, a scampering animal, a little wind in the high reaches. I thought I'd stay in the woods for the night but grew more and more convinced that he'd come back. So I walked parallel to the highway, still at a good distance from it heading in the direction I wanted to go, north.

I walked a while, feeling my breath begin to return to something approximating normal but only approximating it. I was shaken, truly shaken, even more so than the one time back in New York City's hard days of the late sixties when someone pulled a knife on me in Central Park and me and Ronni pushed and then ran. That had felt like someone showing off, like maybe they would grab what we had if they could, but this, this felt different. The intent was not about wanting something I had. I knew in my marrow that his intent was about wanting to annihilate me, to snuff me out, to expunge something from deep in him by getting rid of me. I was still shaking. I hadn't cried though. This was way past tears. Way past feeling sorry for myself. This was about saving myself from what felt like an evil force.

I couldn't spend the night in the woods. I cut diagonally across to the highway and waited in the side dark until I saw a truck at a distance. I came as close to the road as I dared and waved my arms—not putting out my thumb, I wasn't hitchhiking, I was needing help. I was desperately needing help. The truck pulled over, I took a deep breath and decided on trust. I ran up and climbed on the running board and looked into the open window.

It was a young guy, blond, he started to smile at me, to say hello, to ask where I was going, but he stopped. He got quiet and just nodded his head. He took one look at me and he knew, I swear he knew. And somehow, he made me know that he knew and that he would not harm me. He didn't speak any English, and I don't speak German, but he let me know that he was safe and that I would be safe with him. By pointing to his watch and a map he told me we were less than an hour from Hamburg. When we reached the city, he did something unexpected, he took the exit for the university district. He drove his truck into the part of Hamburg with narrow streets not meant for big trucks. He drove slowly and carefully. He drove until he found a well-lit area where lots of college students were milling about, having beers, listening to music. He stopped the truck and people looked up and he must have said "this woman needs some help, someone speak English." He nodded at me that it was ok, and I got down from his truck and in seconds a few people had come up and asked me what had happened. The truck driver waved at me and drove off. I told them just a bit, enough so the women around me came closer. A young couple took me home with them. I had a hot bath, something warm to eat, a safe place to sleep. The next day I took the train to Copenhagen.

PART TWO

THE PARK

ANTONIA MATTHEWS

DAISY'S NINE. HER MOTHER HAS RECENTLY REMARRIED AND now they live in her stepfather's house. She's lonely, missing her neighborhood friends and her mother is busy keeping her new husband happy. He's a stern, taciturn man, and this is his first marriage, he's not used to little girls, and she's shy around him. She's been told to go and find something to do, so, although she's not allowed to go to the park alone she quietly leaves the house and walks up the hill towards the park.

She has to cross the main road, which she's not supposed to do alone, and scrambles up the grassy hill to the park. She loves this park. It's not a park with swings and slides, but a big grassy meadow, and it's like being out in the country even though it is bordered on three sides by roads. There are trees growing close together or scattered across the park, and dips in it which she calls the Dumpties. She and her friends run down them, and then up again, laughing, trying not to fall over. There are also bushes and some of them have brambles where they look for blackberries. The park stretches all the way to the River Avon gorge. When Daisy goes that far, she stands on the first rung of the fence and looks down at the river and beyond to the Welsh mountains, hazy from the coal mines. She used to live in a house nearer the park and she could come over everyday with her friends.

Today, Daisy's just wandering through the grass, pulling stalks and chewing on them As she walks round a clump of bushes, she sees a man lying on his side in the grass, leaning on one arm, and holding a grass stalk in his other hand. He's chewing on it and when he sees her, he smiles and says,

Warm grass tastes good, doesn't it?

She stops and nods her head. She isn't supposed to talk to strangers.

He sits up and says,

Where are you going?

Across to look down into the gorge, Daisy says.

Well what about that, he says.

I've got a daughter about your age and I'm waiting here for her and her mother. We're going to walk to the gorge. Why don't you sit down on the grass and wait for them with me?

He's friendly, Daisy thinks and his family is coming soon so she thinks that is alright, so she sits down cross legged beside him.

Where else do you like to go on the Downs? He asks.

To the Dumpties, she says. *Me and my friends like running up and down them.*

Your daughter and me could do that.

Are you meeting friends here? he asks.

No, I'm here alone, today.

He moves closer to her,

My daughter likes to be tickled. I wonder if you do too,

and he moves still closer and reaches out and pats her knee. Daisy starts to jerk away, but he goes on,

This is where my daughter likes to be tickled,

and he slides his hand up her thigh. She wants to say no, because this doesn't feel right, and she pulls away and tries to scramble up, but slides on the dry grass. He's almost on top of her when she feels a slobbery tongue on her face and a large black dog is jumping around her and the man,

Charcoal, Charcoal, shouts a voice,

and a woman come round the bush.

Oh, I'm so sorry, She says, and starts towards the dog.

But she stops, seeing a small girl pulling away from a man who is lying almost on top of her.

What is going on? She says.

The man is scrambling to his feet and the woman comes toward them.

Is this your father? She asks the girl,

pointing at the man, and looking at Daisy. Daisy shakes her head. She's beginning to cry and tremble; she pulls herself up to sitting and rubs her face on her blouse which has come loose. The woman turns back to the man but he is running away, Charcoal after him.

I know what you are, she shouts after him as he disappears.

I got a good look at you. I'm going to report you!

She turns to the girl, and smiling, sirs down beside her and handing her a handkerchief, gently says,

Can you tell me what happened?

The woman waits, and bit by bit Daisy's sobs stop, and she says, her head down as if she's talking to the ground,

Well, he asked me to sit down beside him, because his daughter would be coming soon.

Yes, and then?

Well, Daisy pauses, still looking down,

he, well he told me that his daughter was ticklish and he wanted to show me where she was ticklish, and he was sliding his hand up my leg. . .

And?—you're doing very well, the woman says quietly.

And then the dog came and jumped on us and licked us, and—well then you came.

She bursts out crying again and throws herself against the woman, who feels that she can hold her now. They sit like this for sometime. Then Daisy says, wiping her eyes,

I was frightened. It was horrid.

Did he touch you anywhere else? the woman says, gently.

No, he'd just begun, and then the dog, and then you, came,

and she holds the woman tighter.

The woman says, *It was frightening and it's alright to be upset and cry.*

Daisy sits up and looks at her, and almost smiles, then she starts to cry again, and blurts out,

How will I tell my mother? Oh she'll be so angry. I'm not supposed to be here or on my own.

So she didn't know that you were here?

No, I slipped out. She told me to go and find something to do. Now that she's married to my stepfather, no one has any time for me.

The woman sits for a while, and then sighs.

She says to Daisy,

Here, I have another hanky so you can wipe your face, and I've got a comb.

She reaches into her handbag, which she had dropped on the grass, and hands Daisy a comb.

What's your name? She asks.

Daisy.

Well Daisy, let's you and I, and look, here's Charcoal coming back, all walk to your home and I'll help you tell your mother.

Daisy blows her nose and pats Charcoal. She looks up at the woman and takes her hand. They both smile. Daisy whispers, *Thank you,* and they turn in the direction of her home.

NYC CHINATOWN

HIROMI YOSHIDA

Mei-Mei and I dragged heavy, weary feet down Chinatown sidewalks—
boredom skewing our colorful Macy's dresses, summer smearing
empty hands. Our busy mouths melted rice paper chewing

Botan candy pulp, sticky be-
tween
tiny
teeth. We dawdled and waited—
waited and dawdled,
for Mama to determine weight of lychees,
price of ginger roots (when we loved

Libbyland TV dinners,
especially the frozen
peas
you stick
on every
fork
prong).

We wanted Papa to end his endless talk with the grocery store owner in some
language we didn't know behind stacks of Chinese newspapers and cigarette
cartons and dried ginseng and Tiger Balm jars.

It looked like our whiny wish would come true, and we'd be
entertained when the stranger
outside the store said, "Hello," with a stringy smile. (Wow! He

sounds like Mr. Sulu!) "Hey,
I want to show
you something. It's over
there, come on."

(Well. . . He doesn't look like the
Bogeyman and he didn't offer us candy). So, Mei-Mei and I trailed
after Mr. Stringbean
with the long hair falling into chinky eyes and the friendly American
voice striding block
after block to ghastly

green-painted tenement
doorway.
"It's behind this door."

I poked cautious
head around
curious corner; eyes spied
pint-sized Tropicana
orange juice carton
smashed onto dirty
tiled floor.

Spread-eagle upsweep—
jack-be-nimble fingers smeared
shame between dangling legs.

"Where's your sister?
Stay right here." I

dared not budge from that
dirty green place. Thick

moths dropped
in the doorway.

Debris of dusk gathered
beneath hairy doormats.

Buzzards ate dogs.

My caged heart
beat flyaway
chicken coop feathers; Runaway

little sister, runaway from
scary yucky chinky guy—run back to Mama and Papa at the grocery store;

fold all thoughts away
(carefully, very carefully)

like today's crumpled
yellow dress—slip through Chinese
laundry steam—it's suddenly
such an easy feat to

stick
frozen
peas
on
every
fork
prong.

IN V. LDS

HIROMI YOSHIDA

When he stepped across the
dilapidated threshold—ruptured
the screened window, did he
see the scrawny girl in the woman
disheveled with sleep? No, instead,
he blindfolded the stars, and taped the
mouths of the flowers shut. I

watched him unfasten
his pants. Will he
spend 7 years on good behavior,
masturbating with the memory
of how he raped me
with the fantasy of consensus—
pulling arms and chairs into askew
positions of compromise? After all, he

dug himself a cinderblock
hole, and buried the deed
with a burglary conviction
quite euphemistically.

It suddenly occurred to me that
"Rape is redemption for woman,"
as I read Sylvia Plath's *Unabridged
Journals* among the wild lilies
at the Cox Arboretum, July 2001;
how Sylvia longed to be
raped by the sun [that killed
Icarus]. This was all

before the done fact [16 years
before #MeToo] when I
accessed the information
that rape was a 1:4 statistic
of namelessly shamed women in the United
States of America. After the fall

into logistical knowledge,
I understood that the
Monroe County Prosecutor
could neither touch nor mend the bruised
mouths and sunken breasts of these
statistical women going the hard way
of nunnery stones, begging us to read
between the squiggly lines
of sex offender registries. Since then, I

compulsively use the Odyssey
Case Management System to search for updated offender
information, catatonic architectures of consensus coalescing and
dissolving, reminding me that justice was

truncated in the evacuated
courtrooms of Bloomington, Indiana.

NEAR RAPE EVENT

DARLENE JOLLEY

IT WAS THE SUMMER OF 1956. OUR FAMILY LIVED IN RURAL Western Pennsylvania. Although I often played with any one of my three brothers on this particular day I was alone.

I had climbed the tree across from the swing set when two boys about the size of my oldest brother, nine years my senior, arrived on bicycles. We talked. Then one boy asked me where my pussy was. I pointed to the porch where the cat was on the steps. the boy said, "Oh no, your pussy is over there behind those bushes. Come let me show you."

I could feel that something was not right, as clearly the cat was on the porch steps. Although I was confused, and *knew* something was not right I did follow that boys command. The other boy got on his bike and was riding away saying, "I can't believe you are going to do that!"

The next thing I remember is lying on my back with my shorts and panties pulled off. The boy/ MAN was coming toward me with a stout penis sticking way OUT! I have three brothers. We bathed together. I was accustomed to seeing them naked. However, I had NEVER seen a stout penis. It was coming toward me.

Suddenly light flashed over me. Then the boy was riding away on his bicycle. He had not touched me. I got up, dressed and walked to the house knowing something very wrong had just happened. I can remember trying in my mind to formulate how to tell my daddy so he could "fix it."

I do not remember going into the house. I do know I NEVER developed the capacity to tell that story until I was in my forties.

Today, now in my adult life, I wonder about THAT LIGHT! That was my guardian angel! I was protected in that very important moment.

What was that boy's experience? Did it change his life? He certainly rode away and

NEVER came back. Does he remember it as an adult? Did his buddy remain a friend ?

THE CAVE

DARLENE JOLLEY

In this writing I want to do my best to put words around one of the most dynamic healing experiences of my adult years.

I believe I have told you that when I went to Penn State in my late teens, time and again I was greeted with, "You have a beautiful smile. What is it that makes you so happy?"

Each time I would hear these words, I would wince. It would be as a shattering of energy within me. People perceived me as smiling. People perceived me as happy. Yet within my breast was heartache so huge there were no words to express what was being held mute, kept silent, hidden within. ALWAYS.

Thus, when I would be told of my smile, I would cringe, wondering, "How can it be that I'm smiling?" "Where is this smile coming from?"? *And* "What do I do with all this hurt I carry everywhere I go?"

Thus began, *or actually deepened to describe it best*, the quest *"Who is the smiling Darlene?"* *"Who is the hurting Darlene?"*

The questions sent me inward and alone, again. Alone to question this personal march into my soul.

The twenties were also *I can now see*, marvelous years filled with multiple activities that gave me light, answers, strength; kept me ever moving onward. I completed my bachelor's degree in Humanities. I thrived in the 1970's in a superbly creative teaching experience in an alternative high school in the Public Schools of Philadelphia, Pennsylvania. I was encouraged to use creativity and new ideas. I developed classes on Hatha Yoga, the use of imagery and meditation for writing and creative expression. I taught Psychology and World Cultures. I brought in quest speakers to enhance the lessons. I developed my own curriculum in the Humanities. This was a teaching mecca.

I also traveled through Western Europe. First with three friends, then once I was comfortable with being in the variety of cultures, I waved goodbye to them. I turned what was intended to be three weeks into a nine-month journey of walks and talks in first Western Europe and then England. I've written a bit of that journey for this group.

During these years of the twenties, I also married a man from Ireland. Thus, it can be seen, in some ways the smile carried me, the pain could be kept at bay enough to engage, enough to participate and YES, enough to even have multiple moments of pleasure.

So there is JOY in the heart of what is ALSO a deep darkness.

I just took a walk away from this writing. This is very eye opening for me to SEE, wow, I was living a creative and fun life while I carried that big boulder of pain.

So, to continue. In my thirties and the simultaneous 1980's absolutely, I can give you multiple, multiple examples of a wonderful creative and dynamic young woman!! However, since it is the healing event of my forties that I want to particularly reveal, I will strive to not get too bogged down with details.

Amidst an exciting and highly creative Master's program in Holistic Health, counseling and education, I was given opportunities to begin to "crack the boulder" and discover the pain that was keeping me feeling separated from life.

The beauty of the Master's program was it included group counseling, personal counseling and it was indeed a program that put into action all that we were learning.

I had an audience in which to voice my heartaches. I was in a program that encouraged the unveiling of our shadows. This program was rich with Jungian and Assagioli psychology. We did multiple segments on dream work and journaling, coupled with music and visual imagery. Yet, I was in an environment that supported all of us revealing childhood dynamics and promoted soul expression and soul growth.

It was when I was in my forties that REAL transformation of this boulder occurred. I began to seriously wonder how much the sexual abuse of my childhood was impacting this hurt that was indeed still going "bump" within me.

I did go to a male therapist who told me that what had happened to me "*was nothing.*" My inner question was, "*If this is nothing, then why does it hurt?*" "*AM I the nothing that is going around hurting?*" "*Why oh why does "nothing" hurt?*"

By this time I was in the graduate program of Boston University. At this time The School of Theology was doing specific studies on sexual misuse within the church. There was a theme of looking to God as "she" and even a rewriting of the Bible with God as "She."

It was in a Biblical counseling course that I first described to my class mate the sexual actions of my uncle and the response of my mother telling me it is what I deserved.

The intention of this particular exercise was to practice NON ~ judgmental listening. My listener asked our teacher and the class, "What happens when you are horrified by what you are hearing?"

Thus Boston University opened up the way to Voice the wrongs of sexual expression in my childhood and youth. Boston University provided counseling and I did have some very good counseling experiences.

I was able to unearth more painful memories. I'll not elaborate too deeply on this but there was a period of time, maybe even years, I can not be sure . . . but there was a period of time when I would walk around and every so often the whip would come up and slash me. The Whip carried the hurting imagery of "and *Yeah, I've been sexually abused by . . . and I would go down my list which by this time had become seven different men . . . I would relive the events . . . and in my minds eye of hurt would be the recognition of and yeah, only two of them were strangers, all of them are either family members or men from the church I attended. The worst of these events is . . . my mother tells me it is what I deserve.*"

Smack would go that whip! Ouch would go my heart, body, mind soul. Into the days activity I would strive to remain while time and again the whip would present itself.

I came to appreciate that what had been more hurtful than the sexual misconduct was that I had not been received as a person. I was a young woman living alone with an abusive mother and the very few men I trusted enough to reach out to, twisted my trust. I could NOT get myself seen!

As time passed the nature of the whip changed. It became that the memories of the sexual abuse would be as a gentle breeze in comparison to the ongoing abuse I was receiving from my mother.

NOW comes the magic!

When I first entered the Master's in Holistic Education one of my teachers also became a best friend. He and his family lived a few blocks from me. When the family traveled they asked me to sit in their home and keep lights and life moving while feeding and tending to their two cats. I've actually written of my experience of being the care giver of their cats when one died.

Gary was a very good friend. That was in the 1980's. It was now the 90's. I was time and again in the malaise of the hurtful poisonous sack that sometimes would almost swallow me. There was an evening when I was having dinner with my friend, Scott. I was talking about my hurts. He said, "Oh, yeah, I hear there's a man that lives on the upper end of Sedgewick Street. I'm hearing that he does a really good job of healing people with sexual abuse."

I knew immediately that he was referring to Gary. I knew that Gary had started a private practice of counseling. I wondered, could he help me now?

So I called him and went to see him as a therapist. It turned out to be the very best therapy I have received ever! The beauty is he knew me in the strength of my dreams and aspirations. He knew me as a friend whose birthday parties he had come to with his family. He knew me as a partner in exploring Truth. I had participated in some of his earliest group counseling efforts. I had been a person he had sought out for advice when he reached a stalemate in these earliest endeavors.

Now I was coming to him bringing this unique chapter of my desire to release myself from the boulder of poison.

He and I entered this new dynamic of healing for the next few years. He allowed me to read my mother's letters. He would mildly say, "She just doesn't get it, does she?"

He was always able to "hit the nail on the head" with his responses to the variety of issues I brought to our counseling time.

Now I will describe that very powerful healing session. He and I had been in therapy for a number of years. We had walked up and down the path of exploring who the variety of abusers had been in my life. We had explored the situations. We had discussed my variety of work roles in this world and what my soul is striving to do. Always I felt appreciative, energized and very deeply gratified by our work.

In the particular session that proved to be so healing I again reviewed briefly, as in an outline, the different life situations of sexual misconduct. Then he had me listen to music so in my imagination I could do with these memories as I wished. What happened was I put all of my memories into a special book with a white leather binding. I was in a deep cave. I walked with this book under a waterfall. I put the book onto a shelf behind the waterfall. I made an acknowledgement that whenever I might want, I could come get my book but I no longer needed the memories.

With that one powerful gift of imagery, I let go of years of carrying a boulder, that now I could release.

My life has been one of ever increasing happiness ever since. Certainly I still have multiple growing edges. Yes, there are still the blank places where I go numb and blocked thus not engaged in what life is giving me all around. But mostly, I am able to enjoy serene happiness a great majority of time. It sure is blissful to know the power of forgiving and letting go!

Today what is important about this is learning to be comfortable with who I am. I want to be free to simply be who I AM. I especially want spontaneity and the ease to simply respond to the life activity that immediately surrounds me.

So today I write this story of that magical moment when we creatively put the episodes behind the waterfall deep in the cave of my heart.

It may be that as I seek to explore who I am in this great world, I just MIGHT revisit some one of those episodes. Do I have your permission to share them?

THE CURE

HÍLDA DAVIS

Girl is attacked in a park on her way
home, then Girl runs home. Girl does
not know if she is hemorrhaging, or
if the red on her hands belongs to
him. She opens the door to her
mother's home, sure to get no blood
on the knob. Girl's crotch, an infinite
ember.

Momma's snores crawl down the stairs.
Momma works 16-hour days, and the
insurance is bad, so Girl never asks to go to
the hospital. Girl never tells Momma when
things are wrong. Even when
the anemia turns her body
into slush.

Girl is Momma's daughter,
after all.

Knows most things
can be healed with honey,
Lemon, and hot water.
Add Vicks, if
necessary.

PLAN B MAY NOT WORK

HÍLDA DAVIS

Girl goes to Harlem to get her things.
Getting your things is the sign that the breakup
is for real. Her ticket to Indiana is one way,
she tells everyone she is going to grad school, but she is running
from blood.

Her old man got a temper. She gets to the door, and
He says *Baby!* and pretends
that he didn't knock the hearing from her skull. He calls
her by name, and when she does not answer,
he squeezes her arm to numbness.
The hallways of the fourth floor walk-up
smell of Dettol; that is how he always cleans up
the fights or nights of sex with other women.
He asks for her body, and she declares her items as hers.
He says *one last time* , and by saying no, she catches
a tongue in her throat. Her old man got
a temper, her old man reduces her to a place
to put his dick when bored.
Her old man can wash her away for a dollar.

Girl does not get her things back.
(Is the breakup for real?)
Girl is thrown out of the apartment as quickly as he came.
Girl uses her last fifty bucks,
walks to one of the new big chain drugstores that plague Harlem's
once brown, delicate face.
Girl asks for a morning after pill and prays.
Girl makes the two hour commute back to her Momma's
house, flies to Indiana two days after.

In her first seminar class, Girl uses the bathroom
breaks to vomit. All she does is sweat and faint.
Girl ran from blood, and now prays for blood.
Girl thinks that stress causes the missed period.
Goes to the doctor, and tells her about Plan B.
Indiana nurse says, *Plan B may not work if you weigh more than 176 pounds.*
Indiana nurse says *pregnant.*
Girl says *termination* without a thought.
Nurse says, *the fetus is a human being.*
Girl says, *me too.*

Two weeks pass.
Girl's decision can only be acted upon
every other Thursday in this city.

The doctor splits Girl's crotch wide with metal,
says, *this should not hurt since you were
ready to open your legs before this.*
Thick, clear, devices connected
to Girl sucking, filling,
bright red the way children
enjoy the ends of Slurpees.

The nurse wraps what could have been
in a blue sheet; runs out of the room
with it. Sometimes, Girl imagines, what grew

inside of her for weeks, still
floating in a biohazard tank, waiting to heal
someone. Sometimes, Girl imagines
The roots of a sycamore tree growing
in a dumpster.

ON HUNGER AND FACING SOMETHING TERRIBLE

HÍLDA DAVIS

IN *HUNGER,* ROXANE GAY WRITES, "IT IS EASIER TO SAY 'SOME-thing terrible happened.' Something terrible happened. That something terrible broke me." She then goes on to share the many ways that she has tried to reconcile this "something terrible."

Terrible things have been happening to my body for the majority of my life. However, I have repressed these things, have done some surface level healing, and have been able to be some semblance of productive in this life. I graduated with honors from a school my high school guidance counselor said I would not make it into. By grace, I earned a Master's degree that I opted to work on as an excuse to leave New York City. I have been able to organize events and hold steady employment. Not many could guess that I experienced trauma unless I shared a part of a life event via poem or social media post. I felt proud of myself for performing the appearance of the wellness or put togetherness that I long for, well. For pushing through the "something terrible." Or, more accurately, I convinced myself that I was pushing through.

Last week, I stood on the scale at my highest weight. I was 236 pounds. I was not upset, or even shocked. I was squeezing into XL clothes, my size 16–18 pants were becoming tighter on my thighs, and I was handed an extender belt on a flight for the first time just weeks prior. I am not ashamed of my body. I understand it as a body, and that bodies change. I did, nonetheless, after seeing that number, watch what I ate more closely and implemented a manageable exercise regimen. However, it was not until I read Roxane Gay's *Hunger* and felt completely seen by her narrative that was I able to identify what caused this weight gain, what spurred my unhealthy relationship with food. After finishing the book, I wrote a note to myself. It reads, "In being more intentional in the ways that I care for myself, I claim that, 'I am here to face my something terrible. I am here because have control of my body.'"

During my undergraduate career at the University at Albany, the organization that a man I once dated, was friends with benefits with, or however you define relationships in college, was a part of, was having a pajama party. I decided to go. I didn't have any close friends in undergrad, but I always found my way of connecting myself to a group or person that I got along with reasonably enough. I looked GOOD. I remember my outfit well. It was a tight fit leopard print negligee. It fell right under my ample hips and backside. My Afro was large, and my twist out cooperated very well with me that night. I opt to wear fuzzy black slippers because at the end of the day, it is a pajama party. I remember feeling great about myself for the first time in a long time, in spite of being heartbroken. This man I once dated, was friends with benefits with, or however you define relationships in college, set boundaries for our relationship and had a new girlfriend. These were all healthy and normal things to do on his part, but heartbreak does not care about what is healthy. When you are heartbroken, you just want to feel better. I just turned 21 that March, so I was able to purchase my own alcohol. I took to drinking rather quickly, and I hardly realized it. I remember drinking in excess the night of the pajama party. Three shots of Bacardi Peach, a full cup of E&J, a grand amount of tequila, capped with a cup of sangria. I made my way to the Campus Center for this event almost a mile away, and I am still unsure of how.

I make a fool of myself in front of everyone. In college, I am not an open person. Nor am I a talkative person. But on this night, I tell everyone I love them. I tell women the truth to their face. "You look so beautiful!" "Your makeup is poppin'!" "Your bundles are right, ma!" I stiffly twerk and dance to the music in my head. I ask for the numbers of men who I find attractive (some of whom I am hilariously still cool with to this day). I see the man I once dated, was friends with benefits with, or however you define relationships in college, with his best friend, and he shoots me a nasty look. I lose the "friends" I intended to come to the party with in the crowd. I am drunk as hell, and I vaguely remember dealing with the burn of tear gas due to the crowd of party goers being too large and unruly according to Albany police.

A young man is with a group of his friends. I have seen him on campus before. I know his name. We follow one another on social media. He seems friendly. He is active in a lot of campus organizations. He tells some people I know that he'll take care of me. They trust him, and he seems trustworthy, so I follow him to his apartment. It is a rather long walk. I do not remember it. I do not even know how I walked for that long in fuzzy black slippers. We stop in a bathroom prior to getting to his apartment, and I throw up. He asks if I am okay, and I simultaneously stumble and say that I am. Once we get to his apartment, I throw up again. Close to his bed. He quickly lifts a shiny silk red comforter so that my vomit would not ruin it. I understood.

I told a person I once lived with about throwing up in this man's apartment, and she asked if it was on a special red sheet that he had. "He'd be so pissed!" That made it clear that he definitely had women in his room before. Which was not a bad thing, or unexpected, but still felt too close for comfort at that moment. In retrospect, his room was a bit seedy and telling of his behavior. Pinned to his wall was a note from a woman that read, "Thank you for helping me, friend!" featuring her phone number. The lightbulb in his room was red. A week prior, I was laughing on the phone with a sister-friend about how men who use colored lightbulbs only use their rooms to fuck.

I knocked out after my body was finished protecting me from alcohol poisoning. This night actually convinced me to stop drinking so much. To date, I have never thrown up so much in my life. I would call it divine intervention, but the following events let me know that that was not the case. I was hanging off of the bed. I was completely out of it. I eventually wake up with him inside of me. I could not move. Everything was spinning. I tried to scream in pain, and he perhaps took it as a moan of pleasure. He used his hand to cover my mouth. I fall asleep again, this time, with my full body on the bed. His arm is around me. I am confused and equally disgusted with myself. Daylight comes and he pulls me on top of him. I am more coherent, and I understand that I do not want this. He finishes. I find my undergarments and quickly walk out of the apartment that he shares with four roommates. I call a taxi and wait in the lobby of the apartment complex for the taxi to arrive and take me to the opposite side of campus.

When I go to him the next day naming what happened, that he raped me, he stated that what I said was loaded. That it was a harsh accusation. So, he made every effort to develop a semblance of friendship with me. He even feigned romantic interest for a long time and tried to convince me that the start of our sexual relationship was not rape, but rather a spontaneous expression of how he felt about me. He did the most to protect himself. To ensure that what happened would never be named for what it actually was publicly. He drove me to his hometown and showed me around. Drove a long way and visited me in the small Newark apartment I was staying in sooner after I graduated from the University at Albany. He would even offer me advice after I finally started dating other people. For a long time, I was convinced that this man was my friend, that he once did a bad thing to me, but that we all do bad things.

This young man and I no longer speak at length. More than five years has passed since he raped me. Because his life has been running smoothly and because I reached out to him as recently as this year, he assumes that all is well with me and that I am okay with what happened that night. We still follow one another on social media, and I am honestly unsure of why. Perhaps I want to keep tabs on him and his location. Perhaps I am in awe of how easily he has moved through life understanding what he did to me. Perhaps he follows me for similar reasons. Through the presentation of the life that he curates on social media platforms, it is evident that he makes a lot of money and that he travels often. He is also dating a very beautiful and small woman. I am still working on loving myself enough to no longer entertain curiosities about whether or not what or who hurt me is still getting on just fine. I am not there yet, at all.

I have no plans of ever pressing charges or ever again confronting this person about the events of that night. Even the way I am writing this protects his identity. I am doing so to protect myself. I have no need or time for the emotional manipulation, as I am discerning, sometimes to a fault, now. I am solely writing this as my own recognizance of a part of what I carry daily. To name what my younger self was not brave enough to accept as a very real part of my narrative. What I carry has now presented itself as a weight gain of about 80 pounds in six years, as well as some toxic behaviors that I have unpacked with the help of therapy and will perhaps unpack publicly at a later time.

In noting my weight gain, I want to be clear that I am not trying to be as small in size as I was in undergrad. I do not hate myself for being and becoming larger. I am honestly pretty okay with being a woman of size at this point in my life. In full transparency, some of the only things about being large that annoy me are how people perceive me, sometimes not fitting comfortably in chairs, my new fear of going to amusement parks, being too broke to buy new clothes for my new size, and how much my ankles hurt and swell by the end of the day. I also found out recently that I am pre-hypertensive, and that I have high cholesterol. But, I do not hate myself for these things. I am writing this entry as a part of a process of openly letting go of things that I carry that do not belong to me.

Something terrible happened. I have repressed and held close this something terrible, and many other terrible moments in my life for a long time. However, in openly naming one of the moments that has troubled me and my Spirit for a considerable portion of my adult life, I believe that I am empowering myself to continue working toward a life that will feel and be lighter.

PART THREE

ESCAPING BEAVER TRAPPER

KALYNN HUFFMAN BROWER

MOST OF MY DARING AND CLEVER HIGH SCHOOL GANG CHOSE the University of Texas after we graduated public school in 1972. While they all stayed in Texas, I chose an adventure to a small liberal arts college in the Pacific Northwest. Just before our sophomore year, I rode with a carload of my friends to Austin to see what I was missing at the big university. We shared stories: My seminar dinners at faculty homes. Their impersonal lecture halls of three hundred or more. True, Austin was a very hip city, still is, far sexier than Tacoma of the 70's. But the monolithic U.T. dorms smelled like locker rooms. I was pretty sure I'd made a good choice.

Then a lightbulb went off. Maybe I wasn't so clever, after all. My friends were all planning to stay in Austin for their sophomore year, which started two weeks earlier than my school. Meanwhile, I'd embarked on the excursion with them, a good four-hour drive, without a plan for how I would get back to my childhood home north of Dallas. What can I tell you? At eighteen I didn't plan ahead. The mantra for our time was *go with the flow.*

I don't remember how much cash I had. It wasn't enough for bus fare. And back then ATMs and debit cards did not exist.

I knew how to hitchhike. Not that I'd ever done it before. But I figured it couldn't be that hard. Of course, hitchhiking could be dangerous, but I wasn't aware of any potential danger to the one thumbing a ride. As far as I knew, any danger of hitchhiking was framed around driver safety and being careful about who to pick up. I didn't look dangerous. It was going to be easy for me to get a ride.

A friendly, old truck driver said he could take me as far as Waco. So I grabbed my rucksack, waved good-bye to my friend Charlie who'd volunteered to get me started, and hopped up into the cab. The weathered cowboy on wheels spit chew and that's a disgusting habit. Otherwise, the drive was boring enough, and before we made it to Waco the old trucker offered to help me find a ride for the next leg of my journey. He got on his CB radio, saying he had a girl who was looking for transportation to Richardson, north of Dallas.

Remember, before we all had cell phones, every trucker had a CB radio that connected him to every other trucker within a 25-50 mile range, depending on terrain and weather conditions. And they all had a CB handle, a code name. So after my trucker sent out the request, somebody responded that he'd heard "Beaver Trapper" was headed home, and he lived north of Dallas. The CB crackled, "Maybe he could give the girl a ride." My driver chuckled, and I couldn't believe my luck. I didn't want to be out on the road alone after dark thumbing for a ride. And, as improbable as it may seem, I had no idea the connotation of the CB handle, *Beaver Trapper*.

I wasn't exactly pure, but I was sheltered, ignorant of how my white skin protected me from many forms of violence. It was a different era. Texas hill country looked like Mayberry. Certainly sexual assault and rape existed, but it was whispered and renamed as something innocuous. Like the standard excuse, *boys will be boys*.

In Waco, the older trucker turned West, while I climbed up into Beaver Trapper's cab. The seats had clean upholstery. Postcards were taped everywhere. "Wish you were here!" and lots of wildlife: bison, roadrunners, armadillos, and, of course, jack-a-lope cartoons. And mixed in were Polaroids of Western art, some of it pretty good.

This guy—I do not remember his given name. Let's call him Trapper for short. He was younger than the first trucker. Not as young as me, but not yet 30, and thank heavens he didn't smoke or chew tobacco. He was funny and easy going in that Texas good old boy sort of way. He had a big mustache and long sideburns. He was a hippy cowboy, kinda cool and fashionable for the time. And, it turned out some of the photos of cast bronze sculptures were—he said—his artwork. Really cool! That's what I thought.

I still don't know if he was truly a sculptor who drove a truck for his day job or if he just gave me the trucker equivalent of "Let me show you my studio," because soon after we crossed the Trinity River and headed through downtown Dallas, he wanted to take me home for the night instead of dropping me off north of the city where I wanted to go. We were on the interstate going 70 miles per hour. How was I going to get out and get home?

Inside Trapper's cab I pressed as far to the right as I could go with the window rolled down, letting the summer air whip my long, blond hair into knots. We sped past mirrored skyscrapers under construction. Trapper man was determined to get me through the city and into farmland where he had studio space and we could have a good roll in the hay. But I didn't want intimate contact with him, especially not in a damn barn.

He was still barreling down the interstate, and it would have been ugly if we'd had a physical fight and he'd driven off the highway. Not that I was thinking strategically about the situation. I simply went with my only weapon: words. I delivered an onslaught of words, mostly about how if I wasn't into it, it wasn't going to be fun for him either. I kept talking louder and louder, and then I started pulling snapshots and postcards off the headliner, throwing the armadillos and roadrunners, one by one, out the window.

That did it. He pulled onto the shoulder, barely coming to a stop, and I jumped into the dust and down the embankment. That's how I escaped the Beaver Trapper.

After escaping Beaver Trapper's cab, I called from the payphone outside the Baskin and Robbins ice cream shop about two miles from my house, and my stepfather came to pick me up. He never asked anything about who'd given me a ride or anything about my trip to and from Austin. Nobody did. Thinking back, it's odd that I never talked about Beaver Trapper to anyone. I was ashamed I'd been so stupid.

So, I forgot about it.

Then I heard a political candidate brag about grabbing pussy. And soon after a friend told the story of her own escape from a serial rapist, also at a tender, trusting age.

Not that rapists only go for the sweet young things. They also attack nasty old women. I'm still not truly safe from the Beaver Trappers of the world.

LA FATALE

JAMES DORR

WAS THAT ALL IT TOOK?

A rag and a bone and a hank of hair, as Burne-Jones' marvelous cousin had put it, a man who had been to India and beyond, writing poems of wonders and foreign lands. Guillemette had seen the painting herself but only some years after it had first been hung, in 1897, the same year Bram Stoker had published his memoir based in part on what *she* had told him. Stoker, like her father Anglo-Irish, had been somewhat of a friend of the family when she was little, which was why later, when she was already on her way to France, she had explained her situation to him.

But Stoker, as she should have expected, assumed what she had told him was only a fiction and, adding his own embellishments to it, wrote it as a novel. Then Kipling, the poet, embellished the painting Burne-Jones had made and titled "The Vampire"—as a penance, perhaps, for his unwise love for the actress Mrs. Patrick Campbell—as if it depicted a natural woman, but one with an unseemly attraction to men, as if it had not been the painter himself who had forced his affection on his picture's subject.

As for Guillemette, born Mina Murray but with a mother from France, grown up able to speak French as if a native, she had fled to Paris, her husband the only other she had told the reason to.

She *was* a vampire.

The "cure," of destroying the one who had made her so, had not been successful. It had been too late. And "a rag and a bone and a hank of hair" was the least of what Guillemette had become.

In Paris she had money. Her husband Jonathan had provided for her when she departed, trying his best to understand. She on her own part began to feel urges, and not just for blood, that led her to a greater understanding of how her friend Lucy had behaved when the poison had taken her. Blood, though, was still required. She frequented butchers' yards, purchasing cows' blood as if to make sausages—having promised her husband she would do her best to avoid harming anyone else through her needs—drinking it later in the rooms she had taken in an inexpensive Parisian suburb.

She was losing weight, however, on this thin fare, thus bony perhaps if not just "a bone." She wore black in the daytime, her face veiled against the sun as if a widow—a "widow's weeds" if one will—as indeed she was somewhat a widow, bereft of her husband and family. These, then, served as "rags." Her hair, though, no mere "hank," grew thick and luxurious, more so than it had been before her ailment.

Her beauty, in fact, despite her thinness appeared to increase. She saw in her mirror—the notion that vampires cast no reflections was nothing more than a superstition—a sparkle in her eyes, dark and deeply set, set off all the more by the paleness of her skin. Her lips, especially when she had just fed, showed themselves a lush scarlet. Her hair glistened raven-black.

But that was not the all. Her longing increased—it was not for blood only. It wasn't sex either, though that was a part of it. True, she had been raised an English Victorian woman, but her mother had still been French. When she was married, she had had no doubt about what she would be expected to do. But it was not just that. She felt restless and listless somehow at the same time.

She made friends among the Parisian women, oftentimes possibly not of the best sort. These new women who, like she, took to darkness, practically living in theatres and dance halls. Guillemette who, in fact, had as a proper Victorian schoolgirl learned music and singing, as well as piano, began to make a living from these places. Often she danced with men between sets as well, often men of higher social station who helped her to advance to better clubs, as well as to find a new place to live in the city itself.

Then one night as she, and a few of the other of *les filles* were returning to their homes, they found themselves stalked by a band of young men. *"Les canailles,"* one of them, Marie, whispered as they bunched together, and then, with a shout, the men were upon them. Another one, Laure, screamed as her dress was torn, while Guillemette felt herself slammed against a wall.

That was too much for her. Shrieking, she fought back. She clawed. She bit. She felt through her teeth the ripping of flesh and the crushing of cartilage, kicking as well, as the world seemed to turn red.

Had she, somehow, fainted?

The next thing she knew, Laure was bending over her. "Are you hurt, Guillemette?" she shouted. "You are covered with blood!"

Guillemette shook her head. "The men. . . ?" she began.

"They have run away," Marie said. "Except for *these* two."

Guillemette rose to her feet with her friends' help and saw, on the sidewalk, the corpses of two men, both with their faces contorted in fear, as if *they* were the victims. Their throats gaping open.

A miasma of butcher shops hung in the air.

"How. . . ?" Guillemette began—but then she realized. The longing, now sated. The joy she felt inside—like sex, yes, she realized, but more than that also.

The fourth woman, Cosette, was sobbing. "You fought them," she said when she got back her composure. "The three of us, we had accepted what would happen, but you did not, Guillemette. It was too dark to see what you did, but in moments it was *they* who started screaming. You must have gotten one of their knives from them—"

Guillemette licked her lips. "These two are dead then?" She looked at the corpses, checking also to make sure none of her own blood had been spilled. "Perhaps it would be best if we told no one of this. *Les gendarmes,* when they come upon these ones, or if the others should go to *them*, they would not believe what we said, would they?"

Marie and Laure and Cosette all nodded. "I'm not sure I believe it myself," Laure said.

"Perhaps we should empty their pockets," Marie said. "The two here, I mean. So if the gendarmes come they will waste their time trying to find out who these 'victims' are."

"I have extra clothes at home, Guillemette," Laure added. "I had better lend you some."

Guillemette nodded. She looked down again. "Perhaps some shoes also, if it would not be too much. At least fresh stockings." She suddenly smiled.

She felt so *alive*.

\#

Later she visited London briefly, a two-night stop on a singing tour. Accepting her failings, she had grown into an exotic beauty, perhaps still appearing a tiny bit frail, but with long, lustrous hair, deep round eyes, a compelling smile, so that she could scarcely be recognized as Mina Harker unless a person had known her well. It was on this trip that she saw the Burne-Jones painting, with the poem displayed at its side.

"A rag, a bone, a hank of hair," she said, half aloud. But flesh and muscle as well, she thought. And nails and sharp teeth. And the will of a hunter—who recognizes that there are ones, sometimes, more evil than even what she has become. Ones who must be rooted out, not just for blood, but for the preservation of those more innocent.

That was le Vampire.

- END -

CARAMEL

TOM BITTERS

AGGIE TOOK ME IN, GAVE ME A PRETTY, RED DRESS WITH short, frilly sleeves and told me to go upstairs and put it on. In two of the rooms, other girls had "dates," but I found an empty room at the end of the hall. The wallpaper was old, pale blue with yellow roses, peeling in places here and there. I went to the window and pulled aside the thin white curtain, tried not to listen to the sounds coming from the next room. Directly across the dusty street, I noticed that the sheriff's office shared space with a general store. Down the street a ways, I could see a ragged-looking brown dog resting in front of a blacksmith's shop, but other than that, there wasn't a lot of activity in the middle of the afternoon. The mining company, where most of the men worked, was up the road a bit, and beyond that, off to the north, the Rocky Mountains rose up sharply, reminding me that I had come a long way. Right below me, I could see three men tying horses to the railing in front of the saloon. One of them looked up at the window, tipped his white hat to me, and I stepped away from the curtain.

I thought the dress was a little tight, but Aggie said it was fine. She stepped back to get a long look at me. I was hoping she would tell me I looked pretty, but instead she said I had nice hands. Then she adjusted my hair, examining a long strand of it in her fingers. "I like the color," she said finally. "How about we call you Caramel?" She pointed to a table where the three men I had seen before were playing cards. "Bring a bottle of whiskey to that table," she said and then kissed me softly on the cheek. "Ask if any of them would like to dance."

The men at the table were more interested in their poker game. Up close, I could see that the man with the white hat wasn't much older than me, almost a boy. The other two were older, never smiled and didn't pay much attention to me, other than to watch me arrange my hair or cross my legs every so often. The white hat man said that I brought him luck especially after he drew a winning card to an inside straight and raked in a big pot.

He was awkward on the tiny dance floor, uncertain of where to place his hands, overly careful not to step on my shoes. With the help of my heels, we were about the same height, and I liked the way he stared into my eyes. When he asked how old I was, I hesitated. "I'm nineteen," I said finally.

He nodded and was silent for a few seconds as he gently moved me around the dance floor. "You dance nice," he said. "But, you don't know how to lie. You're not nineteen." I smiled, and after we stopped dancing I walked back to the table with him. The saloon was beginning to fill up with men who I figured were just getting off work at the mining company. Aggie came over to me, whispered that I should move around to some of the other tables. Shortly after that, I saw the white hat man leave with the other two men. I watched them unhitch their horses and ride off, thinking, *but I don't even know your name.*

A week or so later, the other two men were back. The saloon was crowded that night, and I looked for the white hat man, but I couldn't find him. The sheriff was sitting with Aggie, a sight I'd grown accustomed to. He was the tallest man I had ever seen, lanky, with a bushy mustache and long sideburns. The two often held hands in the saloon and occasionally went for long walks outside. When the other two men called me over to their table, I hoped that they were going to deliver a message from the missing man, but, instead, one of them asked me to sit down. He was much older, forties probably, and he had a noticeable scar running along his right cheek. His skin was dark, from days spent in the sun, and his hair was black and oily, just like his hat. I noticed that he carried a six-shooter with a fancy pearl handle. I'd seen some guns in the saloon, but not ones like this. He took a silver coin out of his shirt pocket, pushed it across the table to me, and nodded toward the rooms upstairs. I looked for Aggie or the sheriff, but their table was now empty. I put the money safely away and followed him up the stairs.

He smelled like whiskey and wet horsehair, and, fully clothed, he sat on the bed and watched me undress, the gun resting on the bedspread next to him. "Why do you need that?" I asked, nodding toward the gun.

He took a long look at me as I slowly began to step out of my slip. "Maybe I'm expecting trouble," he said finally.

"You know something I don't?" Outside, I could hear men arguing and then the sound of a fist hitting a face, followed by some shouting. I started to go to the window, but the man grabbed my arm and pulled me onto the bed.

"You're hurting me," I said and tried to free myself, but he was much too strong. Just then, the second man entered the room, nodded to the other and closed the door behind him. Before I could scream for help I felt a rough hand covering my mouth. My arms were now twisted behind my back, and I couldn't move. The second man picked up the gun and brushed my hair with it. "The way we figure it, Missy, you cost us some money the last time we were here," he said. "And we think it's only fitting that you pay us back." I tried to kick the second man away when he started to loosen his belt, but he laughed, grabbed my foot and wouldn't let go of it.

The more I tried to free myself, the tighter the first man held me down. The other man quickly pulled his pants down, but before he could get to me, there were loud footsteps out in the hall, someone running toward us, and as the door burst open, I freed my mouth and bit the hand covering it as hard as I could. He cried out and let go of my arms. The other man had turned to see who was at the door, and I tried to push him off the bed. The first man had me in a headlock, but I continued to kick, and I felt my foot hit something. I heard the gun hit the floor, and with all my strength I pulled my face far enough away from the man's chest to catch a glimpse of a sheriff's badge. I felt the weight on the mattress lighten as first one man and then the other were yanked off me and fell to the floor. Aggie rushed in, tried to wrap her arms around me, but I pushed her away. Others were now in the room holding the two men down. Still in my slip, I got off the bed. My shoes were side-by-side on the floor where I had taken them off. I put the right shoe on, walked over to the men on the floor and reared back to kick as hard as I could, but for the second time that evening someone grabbed my foot before I could do any damage. The sheriff didn't have to say a word. I could see it in his tired eyes as he shook his head and loosened his grip on my ankle. He seemed to be saying that I didn't belong here, would never belong here, and I sank back onto the mattress, closed my eyes, wondered how long it would be before the man in the white hat would take me away.

STRANGE FIRE

CAROLYN GEDULD

I WOULD HAVE SAID THAT MY DESIRE WAS LIKE A FLAME. BUT that would be the wrong way to put it. In the Bible, the sons of Aaron are consumed by a "strange fire." That's what it was. A *strange fire*. It consumed me.

I met him in a pizza take-out restaurant. We were both waiting for our orders, he a man of color and me, so pale that blue veins were visible through my translucent eyelids. We looked at each other, then without a word, we left the pick-up counter, hurrying to the alley behind the restaurant. There, I climbed on to him, as if he were a firehouse pole. My back scraped against the rough bricks of the building.

When we finished, we returned to the pick-up counter for our orders, without glancing at each other. His name or a way to contact him was not told to me, as mine was not told to him. When I went to my car, I was still throbbing. I missed him already.

But that was to be the only time.

Once home, I went through all the requisite steps necessary for a cheating wife to preserve a twenty-two year old marriage.

"Pizza's on the counter. Don't wait for me. I'm sweaty. Going to shower."

Three times I lathered up, removing his smell from my skin. Then, I went smiling into the kitchen, where my husband and daughter, a college senior home for summer break, were eating. Three slices remained in the pizza box. Although I had less appetite than normal, having been satisfied in another way, I put the slices onto my plate and bit off the end of one. The salty taste of the pepperoni and the silkiness of the cheese reminded me of the flavor of his skin.

Skillfully, I manipulated the conversation away from myself and instead asked about subjects of interest to each of them. *How did the meeting with your new client go? Have you heard from your new roommate for next semester yet?* I was more affectionate than is natural for me, laying a hand on my husband's arm, hugging my surprised daughter good-night.

"Is something wrong, Mom? You're being weird."

"Can't I hug my daughter?"

Later, I had obligatory sex with my willing husband, pretending to orgasm, claiming my grimaces of pain were really delight. *I'll make it up to him. I'll be a perfect wife.*

We lived in a gated community in a mostly-white suburb of the city. It had been somewhat unusual to see a person of color in the restaurant who was not bussing the tables. The few non-white people living in the area were in the professional class. These lawyers, doctors, and bankers wore the clothing and had the speech patterns of the upper class white culture.

Did he? He hadn't spoken, and I hadn't observed what he wore. I only noticed his smoldering eyes. Possibly, he didn't live in the area and was just passing through. People of color had been at the periphery of my vision in my upscale neighborhood—nannies, mowers, window washers. Now it was white people who were at the periphery as I scanned every dark male face to see if it might be him. I took our dog on long walks through the manicured streets, always looking for him on roofs being repaired, in driveways raking new concrete, or getting out of delivery trucks.

At home, my daughter and husband frequently argued.

"You are a bastion of white privilege, Dad. We all are, living here in Waspville central."

"I don't notice you giving your new car or your Apple XR to the black boys downtown who wash windshields for a living, thank goodness. Privilege is what gets you a damned good life and a damn safe one. Not skin color."

Her voice rose in pitch. "Privilege means it's unearned. And people with European ancestry have way more unearned things than African-Americans do. It's a fact, Dad."

"Unearned? I'm working sixteen hour days so we can afford to live the way we do."

The mention of black boys downtown gave me an idea. I'd go into the city. Perhaps I would run into him there, no matter how slim the chances. It was possible. The next time I was alone, I took the Mercedes and drove to the older neighborhoods on the south side. The first time, I just drove around the area, not stopping, looking at the men. None that I saw on the street were him, although I was no longer sure what he looked like. Because the alley had been dark and my eyes had been mostly closed, the only time I had actually seen his face clearly was for a few minutes at the pizza counter. But I felt confident that I would know him if I saw him.

After a few times driving around and tolerating gapes at the Mercedes, I knew it wasn't enough. For my next outing, I parked in a cavernous downtown parking garage, then took a Lyft to the south side.

"I wouldn't walk around here by yourself, Missus, if I was you," the driver said. He was not him.

Because I wanted him to find me as much as I wanted to find him, I had dressed in white as a way to attract his attention. Indeed, heads turned as I, a blond white lady in white, wandered down the area's commercial road, staring into the faces of those who stared back at me. Sometimes, people called out to me or muttered inaudibly as they passed. But I paid no attention to anyone who wasn't him. By the time I had visited the neighborhood a dozen times, I was less of a spectacle. Most people glanced at me, then went about their business. But I was becoming frustrated. He had not appeared in the street. I began stopping in the doorways of stores, then going inside—small groceries, thrift stores with their wares spilling out onto the street, and bars.

Never once did I think I was doing something insane or foolhardy. At home, I acted the part of upper-class wife and mother, cooking meals for my husband and daughter, entertaining friends, organizing the household. When I hired cleaners and gardeners, I chose women or older men. I didn't take the chance of becoming fixated on hired help. I told myself that my secret life was what enabled me to withstand the dull routine of a long marriage. Although I loved my husband, I needed an outlet in order to play my role.

Sometimes, I was careless.

"Have you been drinking?" My husband frowned, sniffing the air around me.

"Yes. I stopped off to see Alice, and we had cocktails. Shall I make you one?"

Most people would have said that in a city of several million people, running into one particular man was a long shot. And that a white woman alone in an African American bar was asking for trouble. I didn't care. A long shot was better than no shot. And the risk only heightened my burning desire.

I was approached in the bars. Men asked if I wanted company. I would say I'm waiting for a friend, which was the truth.

"What's a white lady like yourself doing in a place like this?" I was often asked.

"You need to go home, Lady. It's not a good idea for you to be here," I was bluntly told. I wouldn't answer.

My daughter had returned to college for the fall semester. Just before her mid-term break, she texted that she was bringing a friend home with her. Thinking it was probably one of her room-mates, I was pleased. Several of my husband's friends had been invited to our house for a traditional Thanksgiving meal, including my sister-in-law and her family. Young people at the table would be a welcome addition.

Then she arrived, bringing with her not another girl, but a tall black boy.

"This is Rodney. Mom, Dad. He's my friend."

They were on the front stoop. My husband took a step forward to shake the young man's hand. I took a step back. It was him. Or was it? Was the one I was searching for so young? My daughter's age? But his face, his smoldering eyes looking into mine. Yes. It was him. I was sure, or fairly sure.

Somehow, we were now all standing in the foyer. The front door was closed. My thoughts were scattered, but I hugged my daughter and grinned benignly at Rodney. Ever the good hostess, I showed him to the guest bedroom. He was not going to sleep in my daughter's room. My husband would not have stood for that.

All the while, Rodney politely called me "Ma'am," but I knew he was just being cautious while we were not alone.

That night, in the privacy of our bedroom, my husband spoke to me in a whisper.

"That black boy is not our daughter's boyfriend, is he?"

"She said he was a friend."

"I'm not being a racist. I just don't want her making her life harder than she has to. That's all."

Although I didn't say anything aloud, I agreed that Rodney was not to be our daughter's boyfriend. But not for the reason my husband gave. He was not to be her boyfriend because he was *mine*.

To make sure, I would see what happened the next day. It would be Thanksgiving, the day our guests were expected. I would see if Rodney would give me a sign that he recognized me, that he still burned for me, that he was the same man as the one I had met at the take-out counter. In my memory, at the moment of our meeting, the fire in the pizza oven had flared, causing the servers to take a step back as the heat washed over all of us. Rodney would remember and find a way to let me know.

Now that I knew his name, I said it softly, letting the sound roll over my tongue.

Rodney, Rodney.

While my husband slept, I stayed awake repeating his name, wondering if he was lying awake in the guest room repeating mine, now that he knew it. How startled he must have been when our front door opened, and there I was, his white lady who he never thought to see again. How hard it must have been for him to suppress the instant eruption of desire.

The next morning, while both my daughter and Rodney slept in, I waited impatiently in the kitchen, drinking cup after cup of black coffee. My husband went to the supermarket to pick up last minute supplies for the meal—butter, extra garlic, bags of ice. Mid-morning, I set the oven to four hundred degrees and prepared the turkey, stroking the skin of the bird, pretending it was his skin. Knowing I was alone, I even bent over and licked it, a foretaste of what I hoped was to come. *What would have to come.*

Finally, my daughter and Rodney appeared, wanting coffee and breakfast, which I provided. Then my daughter asked how they could help. I needed a way to be alone with Rodney, so I sent her to the dining room to set the table. Rodney offered to peel potatoes. This, I knew, was a sign. We would be working together, me scrubbing the potatoes, then handing to him to peel. He would have had to have known that this would be an opportunity for my hand to brush against his in the process.

As we went about our task, neither of us spoke. This, too, was a sign. He knew we had to be cautious, that words could give us away, that my husband or daughter might overhear.

Later, my daughter waylaid me.

"Mom, don't do that again."

"What?"

"Make a person of color peel potatoes. It's racist."

"Oh? How?"

"Think about it. It's the most demeaning job in the kitchen. It sets you up as the creative one, the cook, and him up as the lowly servant."

"What should I have done?"

"Like, you could have asked him how he wanted to cook the potatoes. That would have been treating him like an equal."

Meanwhile, my husband had other concerns about Rodney.

"I've put some of your jewelry in the safe with my Rolexes. It's, you know, just to be on the safe side. We don't know anything about this. . . this. . . Rodney. He's so quiet. Our daughter says he is studying physics, but you never know about someone with his. . . his. . . background, do you?"

The doorbell rang. It was the first guest, my sister-in-law, her husband, and the twins, who were in college a couple of years behind our daughter. Soon, the four young people went down to the basement. Strains of the music they liked could be heard upstairs. More guests arrived. My husband served everyone drinks. I brought out appetizers.

I was displeased that Rodney had not offered to stay in the kitchen with me. When everyone came to the table, I made my displeasure known by refusing to look his way while my daughter introduced him to the assemblage. But I glanced at him while my husband was carving.

There seemed to be a sadness in his eyes. He sent what might have been a stricken look in my direction. It melted my heart.

Many times during the meal, I perceived signals from Rodney that he was as anxious as I for a time when we could be alone. The sensual way that he slowly chewed his food, his seductive peeks at me, his full attention when I spoke were all signs to me of his ardor. When the meal was over, he silently brought dishes into the kitchen, giving us the chance to have glancing touches as he handed silverware to me.

Then we were separated for several hours while some went to the family room to watch the game on TV, others went to the basement to play music, and a group went for a walk with the dog. A couple of the women stayed with me to help finish cleaning up and have a glass of wine. Although inwardly it annoyed me to be distracted from my goal, I chatted with them about recent purchases, diets, and remodeling projects using a deceptively lively tone. All the while, I was fantasizing about him, right here under my roof after months of searching, at last available to me.

Finally, everyone left. I persuaded my husband to go to bed before me while I tidied up. But I turned the lights off in the kitchen and sat quietly in there, hoping my daughter would think I had gone to sleep, too. I could make out a conversation between her and Rodney without being able to make out the words. Although he didn't speak much, her voice sounded agitated, demanding.

I dozed off for awhile. When I awoke, the lights had been turned off. It meant that Rodney would be waiting for me in the guest room. Hurriedly, I undressed completely, leaving my clothing in the kitchen. For a second, I thought I heard my daughter's voice coming from the guest room, but then there was silence.

At last, it was time. My skin was on fire. Quietly, I opened the guest room door. It was too dark to see. I closed the door behind me, felt my way to the bed, and slipped beneath the quilt.

PART FOUR

BETWEEN A ROCK AND A DREAM JOB

JANET CHEATHAM BELL

Following is a description of actual events; however, the names of people and places have been changed to avoid embarrassment and possible litigation.

IN 1978 I WAS HIRED BY GANNON & COMPANY, TEXTBOOK PUB-lishers, to my dream job. I would be editing literature anthologies for grades seven through twelve. Since childhood I had loved books and reading. I longed to work with books, to edit and write them. At the time I was the Ethnic Studies Curriculum Consultant for the Indiana Department of Public Instruction. I worked with educators around the state to help them identify teaching materials that would more accurately mirror the world we live in. Because Gannon had been reluctant to make their texts more inclusive, they had lost significant market share to other publishers who had revised their textbooks to reflect the social changes initiated by the movements of the 1960s. During my second pre-employment interview, Ken Cooker, Gannon's president, told me they were planning a major revision of the literature series to add groups that had been excluded—African, Asian, Hispanic, Native Americans, and women.

In ascending order, the team consisted of three editors, an "author" for each book, the program manager, and the director of secondary programs. The "authors" were primarily hired for their resumés; they didn't write or edit anything, but they looked over the editors' work, made suggestions, and occasionally came in for consultations. Each editor was responsible for two books and I was assigned to edit the texts for grades nine and eleven. In addition, I was to provide suggestions for literature by the excluded groups for all six grade levels. A couple of editors on the team were not happy with the direction of this revision, so there was some resentment aimed at me. Sarah told me the only reason I'd been hired was because I was black. Sam, who had managed the literature program for thirty years, refused to have me on "his" team, so he was demoted to editor. Gannon was part of a multinational conglomerate that expected quarterly profits; Sam's bigotry would not be allowed to interfere with their bottom line.

I had not previously worked for a corporation, but soon discovered that it was similar to other office cultures with workers competing for promotions, gossiping to gain some advantage, and being aggrieved by the success of others. These negative energies ramped up during our periodic evaluations, promotions, and especially when there were rumors of pending RIFs. (Their euphemism for layoffs was **R**eduction **I**n Force.) The Marketing and Sales people were the company's stars because they traveled all over the country and were credited for bringing in the money. Editors, the people who actually developed the products they were selling, were considered tedious grunts. However, because of Gannon's interest in getting the word out about the new direction of their literature series, I was asked to advise Marketing on writing promotional copy. I also traveled with the sales force to some of the large urban school districts to help close deals.

Sarah and I were hired at the same time, but I was promoted to Editor ahead of her and she was really annoyed by that. Her bitterness was visible and vicious. What she didn't know was that I had to insist upon that promotion after I closed five of six sales in districts where the decision-makers were adamant about having black writers included in their texts. At a team meeting while we waited for the program manager to arrive, Sarah wondered aloud if it were true that Don (a very productive sales rep) really did sleep with every female he traveled with. She was signifying because I had just returned from a presentation with Don, although we had not traveled together. She also didn't know, and would never learn from me, that in fact, Don was a pimp for Ken Cooker.

Cooker had a reputation (among the few black employees) for liking black women. It didn't take much for him to earn that sobriquet—he openly admired a black secretary who dressed in snug clothing and bold jewelry. And Cooker had taken Margie, the black woman in the personnel office, to lunch a couple of times.

After I had been with the company a few years, Don stopped at my cubicle one day. "Ken Cooker really likes your work."

"Good. I'm glad to hear it."

"You know, with your background, you could be Ken's executive assistant for multiculturalism."

"Who's the executive assistant for multiculturalism now?"

"We've never had one; you would be the first. And it would pay more, a lot more."

When I didn't respond he said, "What d'ya think?"

"It sounds interesting, Don. Let me think about it."

I did think about it. I was making a good salary, but for the first time, I owned a house by myself, which meant I had to hire people for the yard work and any other maintenance that needed doing. I could certainly use more money. But why was Don making this offer? Why hadn't Cooker called me into his office and made the offer himself? A couple of days later, Don visited me again to learn my decision. I told him the truth.

"You know Don, I really like being an editor, and I expect to become a senior soon. I don't think being Cooker's multicultural assistant will help with that."

"Really? Are you sure?" Don seemed surprised, but he didn't try to change my mind.

Either Cooker was not satisfied with my answer, or Don decided to try another approach. A few days later, he came back.

"You know, Janet, you could really do well for yourself as Ken's assistant. You could double your salary, travel. . . ." His voice trailed off anticipatorily.

When I didn't respond, he said, "You know Ken really likes black women."

There it was. I couldn't believe he had actually said it.

"Ken likes black women?" My voice rose with incredulity. "How can you tell? Where are the black women program managers? There are no blacks on the editorial board; only three black women working in a professional capacity in the whole company, and two of them, including me, are overqualified for their positions."

Don was standing in the entrance to my office cubicle, and I was sitting at my desk. I stood up because I wanted to look him in the face.

"I *hope* you're not saying Ken Cooker likes black women in the way white men *usually* like black women—behind closed doors with their legs open."

Don usually had a smooth demeanor and was quick with a retort, but he dropped his eyes and left my cubicle without another word. He never mentioned Ken Cooker to me again. Nor did Cooker ever say anything about an executive assistant for multiculturalism.

"I WANT TO GO HOME. NOW!"

MARIA HAMILTON ABEGUNDE

PRAISE TO OLODUMARE. HONOR TO MY ANCESTORS. PRAYERS to all the orisas who guide my journey, especially the orisa Osun. Maferefun Osun for walking with me this path, for helping me to remember the words that in another life set me free; and for being the healing balm to help me bear the consequences of choosing to be free.[1]

As I finished this essay, the hearings for the new supreme court justice were taking place. I chose to not listen to or watch the live sessions of testimonies, questions, and rebuttals, even those of Dr. Christine Blasey Ford. However, the following morning, I listened to the replays on NPR. As I did so, a wave of urgency passed over me, followed by a grounding calm. In the end, I knew what needed to be done. The words, *believe her, believe her, believe her* came as a whisper through my back, the center of my heart chakra.

---

1. When my healing gifts began to emerge, I came to understand and have confirmed that in a past life I had survived many Middle Passage voyages, the first of which was during the mid-sixteenth century from what is now Nigeria to what is now Brazil. On that voyage, I screamed the word "No!" to a crew member as he tried to rape another woman. I had learned this word watching the chiefs negotiate with the white men who came to buy us. That word would cost me dearly in all my lives. This story would become the foundation of my healing work and the basis for my research and scholarship at both the MA and PhD levels. It is told in *The Ariran's Last Life: A Memory Work,* an excerpt of which can be found in *The Kenyon Review,* Winter 2008 and in *Best African American Fiction* 2010.

Five days later, I listened to NPR again, this time to the replay of
the mocking of Dr. Ford at a rally; her "I don't knows" thrown out to the
audience as they laughed, as if a few days prior she had not gathered her
courage from every part of her soul to stand before men (mostly) and
millions of people (virtually) to tell the story of a part of her life she'd
rather not have happened and would have forgotten if she could have.
This time, no words whispered themselves to me. But, a sudden anger
filled my chest. Tears followed. It is the first time in a long time that I
have been so angry. Yet, anger is too simple a word for what I was feeling;
it is the best word I have to describe the overwhelming and uncontrol-
lable weight and heat that rushed into and settled inside my chest. It is
the same feeling—despair?—that settled in my chest while watching
the video of the murder of Philando Castile two years after his murder.[2]

I expected most of what happened in response to Dr. Ford's alle-
gations: the disbelief by other women about her memory, the discard
by men for her refusal to forget, questions about her integrity, and the
bureaucracy of a perfunctory investigation. In 1992, when I dared share
publicly for the first time about incidents in my life, there were moments
like this. I, therefore, very early guided my feelings into creating col-
laborative healing work and spaces for anyone who needed them. But,
that morning, I was struck by the public retort. No memories emerged
for me; yet, I could not stop wondering how Dr. Ford felt—and all the
survivors/victims of violence who have been/are being laughed into
silence and the shadows.[3] I wondered about how the new permissions
that have been given to scoff at someone else's pain will shape how we
address trauma as a society. I wondered, too, if only visible, completed,

---

2. On July 6, 2016, Officer Jeronimo Yanez pulled over and shot to death Philando
Castile, a 32-year-old Black man who was driving in Falcon Heights, MN. Before reach-
ing for his license and registration, Castile informed the officer Yanez that he had a fire-
arm. As instructed by Yanez, Castile did not reach for his firearm. Diamond Reynolds,
Castile's girlfriend and her four-year-old daughter were in the car when Yanez shot Cas-
tile seven times.

3. I am aware of the ongoing discussions of whether the words survivor or victim
should be used and how both can cause further injury. Survivor can conjure images of
conquering, super human resilience, and healing. Victim (unlike victor) can conjure im-
ages of perpetual helplessness.

and provable traumas with evidence would be accepted into the public and/or collective narratives and by whom?[4]

Of course, as a Black woman, I could not help wondering what, if anything, had changed for me and other Black and Brown women in the world. I was in my 20s when Anita Hill testified against Clarence Thomas. I remember how poised she needed to remain, answer questions about what had happened as emotionless as possible. I remember how her choice of clothing, a sky blue, reflected a calmness, nothing strong and powerful as black, gray, or navy. She was Ms. Betty Jean Owens 32 years later, willing to sacrifice her personal safety, and willing to field questions that insulted her womanhood and race, to tell the truth and keep her dignity. I cannot help thinking that a Black woman testifying against a Black man about to be appointed to the highest court in the country is not the same thing as a white woman testifying against a white man in the same position.

But, if I ponder this too long, I will need to write another essay: the raping of a Black woman, although the rape of a woman, is not perceived the same as the raping of a white woman by anyone. The histories of slavery and lynching teach us this: terror and resistance shaped and continue to shape our lives simultaneously. When I began writing this essay, Tarana Burke had already said out loud "Me Too" and founded the Me Too Movement twelve years before #MeToo emerged as a hashtag. In addition, Darlene Clark Hine's 1989 essay, "Rape and the Inner Lives of Black Women in the Middle West" was an essential part of my teaching on Black feminisms, womanism, and the sexual lives of Black women. In this essay, Hine argues that due to racial, economic, and social tensions and histories that Black women had developed a culture of dissemblance, an intentional and necessary secrecy about their inner lives that shielded them from public scrutiny and attack. Hine writes further that: "... rape and the threat of rape influenced the development of a culture of dissemblance among Black women."

---

4. In *The Body in Pain: The Making and Unmaking of the World*, Elaine Scarry suggests that one of the reasons why torture and other forms of violence are so effective is that often there are no visible scars, no ability to articulate what has happened and what cannot be seen by others.

I did not read the Hine's essay until I taught it for the first time as a graduate student one June. By that time, for over twenty years, I had already written about, published, and taught about the sexual violence that had occurred in my own life, beginning at age six and lasting for nine years. Very early in my life I realized that secrecy about my suffering would lead to my emotional, psychological, and spiritual pain. Even more so, based on the examples in my life, denial of my suffering would lead to an unhappy and joyless existence. This was important to me: at age 15 I decided that I wanted to be happy for the rest of my life and no longer controlled by the fear of someone knowing what was being done to me. I am grateful that I came of age at a time when cell phones and the internet did not exist. Had they, without a doubt, I would have died from having to experience daily the very public nature of the violence done to me.

The first time I read and discussed the Hine's essay with students, who themselves were coming to terms with their own sexualities and violence, I understood her argument in a very real way and what was at stake for Black women when they spoke the truth about their lives. That summer, I also read Danielle L. McGuire's "It Was Like All of Us Had Been Raped: Sexual Violence, Community Mobilization, and the African American Freedom Struggle." In that essay, McGuire details the rape of Black women, their choices to testify against their white attackers, and the protections extended to Black Womanhood under the Civil Rights Movement. Two incidents remain with me: The 1944 rape of Ms. Recy Taylor of Alabama by six white men, and her immediate disclosure to her father, husband and the deputy sheriff after the rape; and the 1959 rape of Ms. Betty Jean Owens of Tallahassee, Florida, by four white men. In Taylor's case, the Grand Jury failed twice to bring indictments against the men. This is why the following stand out to me in the Owens story: the arrest, conviction, and life sentences of the men and Owen's decision to appear in court and testify against them.

Reading the essays made me consider how similar experiences may have limited the actions and responses of the adult women I tried to tell about my sexual abuse as a child. I also began to think about the responses I had received from audiences when reading poetry about my experiences.[5] These two essays and the stories in *Love with Accountability: Digging up the Roots of Child Sexual Abuse* edited by Aishah Shahidah Simmons reconfirmed what I knew: all my life I had done the right thing: told my stories any way I needed or wanted. In the beginning, I wrote mostly for myself: I wanted to document each incident. In the event I ever doubted myself, I could refer back to my own handwriting and voice to tell me the truth. I also told my stories for anyone who could read or listen to them: these are hard stories and telling them does not get easier; nor does it seem there will ever be a need for their end.

This last fact saddens and frightens me for multiple reasons. Sexual violence continues to plague our communities throughout the world. Some weeks I hear stories so frequently I want to run to the river and take everyone with me and bathe them. And, there is this, too: the healing that has occurred in my life—that allows me to live fully and joyfully as a sexual being, because sexual violence at all ages and levels steals pleasure, substitutes pain and shame instead—my healing belies a deeply troubled past that I don't hide but also don't speak openly about because it is the past and, as a child, I decided that what had been done to me by both men and women would never define my life. When people look at me, they don't want to (cannot) imagine that my life has been anything other than what it is. Many cannot bear witness to me or my experiences. However, what and who I am this moment in time is a direct result of the deep pain and violence—the renting of my body and life—that I experienced and my insistence and ability to make meaning out of them. Documentation such as this essay is evidence of resilience and resistance in the face of extreme life circumstances.

As a healer I am conscious of this moment in the world and the opportunities I have been given during this new cycle of revolution, birth, and healing to reflect on my life in a new way, one that helps me better

---

5. When I began reading my work in public, audience responses included turning away from me and asking me: *Why you have to talk about that in public?* Others, primarily women, responded by sharing their own stories and this led to groups of us in the 1990s leading healing workshops for women. The role of men in this discussion, including my father, is a future essay.

understand myself as I enter my second century. For example, I am grateful that this moment in time allows *Love with Accountability* to breathe and reach thousands. As someone who never named my abusers and rapists, I read these stories about naming and truth telling—and love—with peace and knowing that these were people who had reclaimed their lives in ways so many could not.[6] Their stories—my stories—are not separate from the ones told by Hine, McGuire, others. They are part of historical and political experiences that have and try to silence women about what has and is being done to their bodies and souls at ages so early one must wonder how many of us physically survived, only to be raped again as adults.

Because of my history, child sexual abuse and rape (at age 15 and 16) are connected, part of a continuum of how girls and women, the female, feminine, or feminized body, are treated and what they are expected to endure. An essay on unsuccessful attempted rapes, therefore, makes all of this resurface. Certainly the question for some might be if that history led me to be more susceptible to being raped as an adult, as if there is a battery of behaviors, criteria, and costuming to determine this. This moment in time, with access to stories and healing, is the perfect time to help, in particular, young women understand that *a luta continua/* the struggle continues and that everyone knows someone who has been wounded in this most heinous way. Even if an attempted rape was unsuccessful, we have still been wounded. How do you learn to trust yourself or someone else ever again? How can you trust that your desires and fetishes—your freak—is just because you like to feel something new and not a result of an unidentified experience? How do you joyfully choose what to wear to feel good about yourself and, yes, sexy as you define it? How do you ever believe that it is possible to have pleasure and joy

---

6. As a child, the initial responses to my trying to tell silenced me. At the age of 6, other circumstances made me believe that I would be "in trouble" for what was happening. Later, I would realize that would not have been the case, and that my life might have been different. By the time I began publicly sharing what had happened to me, I also knew that all those people responsible had come to no good end. Moreover, I wanted the focus to be on me, the girls and women who had been harmed, and the healing we needed.

without the fear of boundaries being broken, your body being beaten, your soul being killed?

When the #MeToo campaign rolled onto my Facebook page, I did not hesitate. I did not detail, but I did not second guess adding the hashtag and sharing that I, too, had been wounded in this way. When the invitation for this essay appeared, I did not hesitate. It requires details, but I have become accustomed to sharing them. Here is one such detail about one part of my life that I always want to remember.

This is my story.

I was a freshman at a Big Ten university. It was my first semester. I had neither boyfriend nor girlfriend. I met men and women at parties. We went to dinners, the movies, or university events. These were often group activities, but occasionally dinner was private.

The evening I am recalling was such an evening.

Weeks before that night, I had started "talking" to a guy. Based on his interactions with those I was getting to know, I felt safe. Based on my life experiences, I was careful with whom I chose to be friends or intimate partners. As a freshman, I understood I had to protect my reputation. I trusted my instincts. So far, they told me this guy was okay. In addition, the grapevine and gossip tree had not revealed any horrid stories.

When he asked me to have dinner, I accepted. When he suggested his apartment, close to campus, I accepted. I do not remember if I told my roommate or anyone else where I was going. That evening, he came to pick me up: We rode the train together. The walk from the train to his apartment was not far. It was a warm fall night; there was no need for jackets. And, although we did not know each other well, we had been getting to know each other rather nicely over the phone. The conversation as we walked was light, the kind you have when you like someone but are unsure what happens after the first date ends.

We arrived at his apartment. I remember it was adult in a way dorm rooms and off-campus university residences were not: clean, organized, a separate kitchen full of plates and glasses organized on shelves, a separate living room with a couch and bookcases, a dining table with place mats, and a separate bedroom. It was comfortable and welcoming, and it smelled good. He had started preparing dinner before meeting me. Tomatoes and vegetables permeated the air.

Nothing fancy.

(Amazing: the things you remember. Our memories are shaped by so much: our peculiar penchants, what interests and surprises us, what causes us love and satisfaction, or what causes us fear and agony.)

We talked for a bit more then he excused himself and went to the kitchen, leaving me in the living room to look around and relax. I was doing just that until I realized he was on the phone, talking to someone in a low tone that I would have missed had I not been sensitive to changes in sound. Something in his voice troubled me and I began to pay attention.

I heard him say, "Man, why don't you come on over. . . " Then he laughed. My psychic and clairvoyant gifts were just emerging, but I suddenly had an image of the other person, bearded, older, also laughing. They were sharing a joke from which I had been excluded. Yet, I was the guest. My entire body tensed. I wanted to run. Instead, I remained on the couch and strained to listen to the rest of the conversation through the sweet smell of the food, the ordered space, and the fear that something was wrong and that I was in danger. Finally, he hung up the phone and returned to the living room.

I jumped off the couch, stood up, and yelled: "I want to go home. Now!"

I remember that we were standing about twelve feet apart. I had to pass the kitchen to get to the front door. The kitchen had a window, looking onto the street below. (Could I jump out of it safely? Without breaking too many parts?) He was closer to the kitchen and door than I was and looked confused. Afterward, I realized that I probably looked like a "mad" woman, yelling for apparently no reason, after weeks of planning, that I wanted to go home. Yes, because I did not know when the other man would arrive—only that he would arrive—I was at that moment a madwoman: a woman willing to move fast and use violence if necessary; a madwoman with a super-heroine ability to know that when the other man arrived, I would not be able to leave.

"What?!" he asked like he wanted to slap me.

"Who were you talking to?" I asked.

"A buddy of mine." There was no mention of the invitation.

"I want to go home!" I yelled again and began moving towards the door.

I didn't run. I didn't know if doing so would initiate any action on his part. All I knew was that I would fight him. He was taller than I was, but not bigger.

For a moment, he looked frustrated, disappointed, like I had spoiled his evening. "I'll take you home so you don't have to ride the train by yourself."

"No," I said.

"At least let me walk you to the train."

"Fine," I said and headed towards the door as he returned to the kitchen to turn off the stove.

The walk back to the train, at the train station: we said nothing. I boarded. I arrived home. I breathed. I may have prayed. He didn't call. I never saw him again.

Weeks later, I mentioned what had happened to a guy I would learn was one of his fraternity brothers. His response was so matter-of-fact: oh yeah, they have a reputation of raping women on campus; together.[7] I had, apparently, escaped what had happened to others and, possibly, saved my own life. All the *men* knew about it. And the women? Over time I would learn that the women were ashamed and shamed into silence; in addition, they did not want to get these young black men into trouble.

> (Pause. Breathe.
> Remembering makes you say again: What the hell?:
> "'Oh yeah, they have a reputation . . . together.'"
> It makes you remember anger and how good you were at controlling it
> to save your life,
> an art form you would perfect into a diamond-edged blade
> to cut your way out of anything that threatened your life.
> Breathe. Pause.
> Remembering makes you wonder

---

7. At this writing, it is impossible for me to explain all that I have contemplated about the silence of his fraternity brothers and their complicity in the harming of young women.

how many women
were unable to trust their madwomen,
or didn't know they had one,
or who were raped / killed
and the screams of their madwomen
were stifled / swallowed / unheard / ignored / buried.
While they smelled tomatoes boiling.
But, I digress.)

This is my story. My story defines me.

When I read the call for submission for this anthology, my dilemma was not whether or not to submit something. No, the question was which one of my stories would I share, how would I share it, for what purpose or for whom, and after so long how would sharing this story serve my communities and contribute to making us free and keeping me free? More importantly: would a story about a rape that was being intuited, not one where there was an overt threat of rape, be the "right" story to share? I was not, after all, touched or verbally assaulted or harassed. Would a story that relied on the narrator's own self-knowledge and intuition be relevant to anyone? After all, women, children, the underrepresented [fill in the blank] are encouraged to doubt what we sense, feel, and know in the bottom of our stomachs. We are deterred from making meaning of the raised hair on the backs of our necks.

I chose this story because at that time in my life, aside from the precognitive and paranormal experiences about the death of my mother, there were few other events that told me to trust who I was becoming and the things I could not see.

I am a healer. I tell others that their stories do not define them. But this story, unlike the actual rapes, abuses, and assaults that predated it, does define me. It is not because I was not raped.

[Does the word rape make you uncomfortable as you read it more than
once? (Yes.)
Does this change how you think of me or might look at me when next
you see me? (Maybe.)

Are you trying to avoid feeling what you are feeling? (No.)
(But, you know you want to.)
Are you reinterpreting everything I've ever done or said? (Stop.)
Keep reading. (Please.)

OR

Perhaps my story is your story and it makes you remember that story
you want to forget.

If so, close these pages now.
Breathe.
Remind yourself: Memory is not your enemy.
Remind yourself: You are alive.
Say. Out Loud: I. AM. ALIVE.
Remind yourself: Someone wrote a story about what happened to her.
Remember: There are more stories.
Know this: The story you are remembering is yours to do with what-
ever you want.
Then, re-open these pages in an hour, tomorrow, a week, next month,
in a year.
Read.
Or never open them again.
Whatever your decision, remember: It is your decision to make.]

More than thirty-five years later, I remember, I recall, I tell. As I have
done from the beginning. While I do not live with this story in the same
way I live with the other assaults, and while this one does not linger in the
shadows, occasionally disrupting an evening, forcing its way into dreams
or conversations, this memory has not disappeared. Unlike the others
that I worked very hard to heal, to put on the page so that they could be
heard, this one, I've kept to myself. I don't want it to go away. Because
even if you are like me and you have walked away alive from serial pe-
dophiles, potential rapists, and actual rapists, there is no escaping what
happened or what was allowed to happen. There is no forgetting that in

the United States, one out of every six women has been a victim of an attempted or completed rape.[8] Of those, college-aged women are three times more likely to be raped than women not in college. More than fifteen million women. When you consider (and you must) that young boys and men are raped, and that Black, Brown, and transgendered people are at higher risks, you begin to understand the magnitude of this violence and its increasing impact on public health. But I digress. Again.

This is my story. My story defines me. I want to remember it.

That night was the first time I used my sixth and seventh senses. It was the first time I would challenge a man out loud with my voice and decide that the size and weight of my body were weapons to be used no matter what the outcome. It would be the first time I knew I would always choose to fight—by whatever means I had. It was the night I knew that although I had lived through all the other things that had been done to me, that from this point on I had the power to demand what I wanted, speak it into being, and to live without fear.

I want to go home now!

That year, I decided I would tell all my stories to anyone who would listen. I would not publicly share them in writing until after graduating from college.[9] When I decided to do so, I called an elder, invited her to my house, and showed her a full-length manuscript that would become *What Is Now Unanswerable*. After reading the poems, here is what she said (more or less): Publish it. I have witnessed this in my church. (I do not remember what else she said about some of the congregation trying to expel the minister and others supporting him.) It would be the

---

8. http://www.rainn.org

9. During my senior year, I began the core courses for my concentration in writing. It was Janet DeSaulniers' generous and nonjudgmental reading of my reflective assignments that allowed me to work through my life and my reasons for writing. Her responses, like those of Gwendolyn Brooks, shaped how I make and hold space in my classroom for others who may need to tell the stories that should not be told. (See "A Lectio Divina for Gwendolyn Brooks: Honoring the Ancestor, Contemplating Healing" in *Obsidian: Literature & Arts in the African Diaspora*. University of Illinois. (Winter 2018, Vol. 43, No 2).

first and only time I would ask permission to publish and make public anything I wrote.

Since "the beginning of time" women have been asked to keep silent, to let others speak for us. For those of us who choose to speak, too often our channels for speaking are blocked or removed. All of us have courage at one time or another to speak our truths—before we experience the fear of repercussions. If we have pushed past that fear, we are then punished as if we are badly behaved children disobeying our parents, or as if we are criminals.

The one thing, however, of which I have always been certain: for me, silence was not an option even when it meant being called a liar or being blamed. I would learn this from Audre Lorde many years later: My silence would not—could not—protect me. The other thing I know for sure: Without writing, I would not have lived. I would not have understood the power of language to break silences about whatever we are told to keep silent about: our victimizations and abuses, our family secrets, our chosen lifestyles, our loves, our desires, our dreams. Our rapes. And the truth.

Truth: Just like when I was a little girl, my "community" knew. And still the women were silent and the men said yeah, they have a reputation. *They knew.* You may think that I am speaking about this community only. I am not. That knowledge made me take an oath: I would not be silent about what had happened to me. I would not ignore what was happening to others. I would help others heal when possible.

The healing is the hardest part: it comes with additional truths we don't want. Someone I thought I could trust—that people led me to believe I could trust—planned to rape me with someone else. It is only because I overheard one side of the conversation—and the laughter—that I learned of his plot. But there is another truth. If someone thought about raping you and attempted to rape you—planned it, started it—there is no escaping the fact that someone plotted to do you harm. After many years of teaching about memory, trauma, and healing and helping women heal from trauma, I know this to be true: Survival is relative. No one except the rapist escapes being raped or survives being raped. Not you. Not your community. Your future partner. Your children. Their children. Not even witnesses to testimonies. Each time we tell, read or listen to an account, we re-experience what happened: It is, yes, as if all of us were raped again.

If you have read to this point, thank you, *obrigada, gracias, shukraan, modupe, adupe.*

This is my story. My story defines me. I want to remember this story. It is my responsibility: the story and the telling of the story. I tell the story to be free.[10] I tell the story to help others get free.

When the story is one of trauma, one must find a way to tell the truth without intentionally harming the reader. They must find a way to offer hope and the possibility of healing without appearing to be matter-of-fact or arrogant, as if every day you get up from beneath your rapist(s) and live. These responses can be signs of deep trauma and shock. They owner and teller of the story must clarify why they wants to tell the story. With that mission in mind, I would like to offer a few things about my own healing process.

I chose this story because although I am no longer a student, I have returned to a college campus. I know without asking, being told, or reading the newspaper headlines, that the young women, men, non-binary, and other gender identified groups around me are being raped, sexually assaulted, or harassed in numerous ways. I know that challenges to Title IX could endanger many more. And, despite Dr. Ford, Me Too, and #MeToo, women and girls still doubt the validity of their stories and the truths of their own experiences.

The responses to questions I am most often asked about my life are these: Trusting my instincts; trusting what I could not see; choosing when, to whom, and why to tell my story; never accepting blaming or shaming. Last but not least: defining for myself who and what I want.

Trusting my instincts. My freshman year in college was the year my gifts of knowing fully surfaced. This incident was the first in a series that would teach me to trust everything that my body was telling me. That night, I heard, felt, and reacted without thinking. If I had been wrong, I would have apologized. But I wasn't. I learned that night that letting out

---

10. Tracie D. Hall. Private Conversation. 2014

my madwoman disoriented my would-be attacker. His surprise at my request and refusal to disclose the conversation confirmed what I was feeling. When I listened to my body's initial message and connected it to what I was thinking, I better attuned to my own needs for safety, love, compassion, space, and time.

Trusting what I could not see. There was no evidence. At least none that people were willing to share until after something had happened. Fear and shame are powerful emotions that can effectively prevent anyone from acting, myself included. To walk away from this incident without being touched, I had to trust my interpretation of events based on overhearing only part of a conversation. There was no evidence of another man, only those words. There was no evidence that I would be attacked, only my interpretation of the contexts before me. When I learned to choose my own interpretation first, I also chose to make meaning of what was before me in a manner that was relevant, life affirming, and life saving for me.

Choosing when, to whom, and why to tell my story. After the incident, I did not know to whom to speak. I started to ask around if anyone knew anything else about this guy. Finally, one of his off-campus fraternity brothers told me the truth. He was the only one. When I chose to ask the difficult questions, I trusted that someone would tell me the truth. In the future, I shared my experiences with an elder I trusted. I had paid close attention to this woman to know that she would listen, support me, and pray with me.

Choosing my words and audience. I chose nonfiction instead of poetry, my preferred genre for most things, because I wanted there to be no mistake: I am the narrator. I survived being raped and a rape attempt. I learned a long time ago that writing or saying these two things together would not kill me. Others were uncomfortable and said sympathetic things, or advised me to move forward; or my story shocked them into silence for a myriad of reasons, including that it activated their own memories of rape. In all cases, I learned to be compassionate with those who listened to me and those who spoke to me. I learned, most of all, to be compassionate and loving with myself.

Never accept blaming or shaming from yourself and others. Those who wanted to and were able to help me did so without judgement or need for reciprocity. I was not mad at those who could not do this. Those who were shocked: sometimes in telling our story we become a mirror or recording for another. Our words and stories have the power to alter our lives and the lives of others.

Once—because other times I could not—once I narrowly "escaped" being raped.

I am here. Alive. Thriving. I am not silent. I am not invisible.

I have learned to define and redefine myself. Words and names are important. Nouns and verbs are important. I have learned to choose the words that describe my experience without hiding what happened.

Do I remember the man's name? No. But, I do remember what he looked like, a lighter brown than I, with a short afro. Do I remember the name of his fraternity brother who told me the truth? Yes. Christopher. Do I remember the building? A yellow brick apartment building on Central Street. It is no longer there. Do I remember the train stop? Yes. Central. Do I remember the near-by restaurants? Yes. Mustard's Last Stand. Two years after this incident, every Sunday I would walk the few blocks and eat their charbroiled hamburger with cheddar cheese.

Indeed, it is amazing, contradictory, surprising, even, what we remember. No matter what that is, believe yourself, especially when no one else believes you.

As I contemplated how to end this essay, I listened to an interview with Bessel van der Kolk. In it, he discusses "How Trauma Lodges in the Body" and what it means to heal from trauma. In his book, *The Body Keeps Score,* van der Kolk writes that one way to heal from trauma is to "own yourself fully." What he writes about healing from trauma is worth quoting in full, especially because I recognized after reading it that what I was feeling that morning listening to NPR replay the hearings and retorts was the "crushing sensations in [my] chest" and the horrible feeling that I was being asked to remember and speak about things I no longer wanted to write or teach about to anyone. But, that I had a responsibility to do so.

"What makes your resilience to trauma is to own yourself fully. . . to separate your sense of yourself from the abuser or trauma. . . ." ". . . you need to feel that feeling. You need to know what is happening in your own body. . .

"Nobody can "treat" a war, or abuse, or rape, molestation, or any other horrendous event, for that matter; what has happened cannot be undone. . . .

But what can be dealt with are the imprints of the trauma on body, mind and soul: the crushing sensations in your chest that you may label as anxiety or depression; the fear of losing control; always being on alert for danger or rejection; the self-loathing; the nightmares and flashbacks; the fog that keeps you from staying on task and engaging fully in what you are doing; being unable to fully open your heart to another human being.

Trauma robs you of the feeling that you are in charge of yourself, of what I will call self-leadership. . .

The challenge of recovery is to establish ownership of your body and your mind—of your self. This means feeling free to know what you know and to feel what you feel without becoming overwhelmed, enraged, ashamed, or collapsed."

To own myself fully. This is the answer to the question people are afraid to ask me: How did I heal from not only this attempted rape, but the childhood rapes? How does one "own herself fully" after such traumas—direct physical wounding to the bodies of one's self and the subsequent spiritual, emotional, psychological woundings? Is healing possible?

Reading this mandate—own yourself fully—made me reflect on my life and the coping/defense mechanisms I created to feel and be safe. In that room, how did I know from a secret phone conversation that I was not safe? I realized that long before being in that apartment with the scent of sweet tomatoes permeating the air, that I had chosen to feel and that I had decided that I wanted to live fully, unafraid of being touched, unafraid of my own pleasure. I wanted to be free of the people who had hurt me and the men like the one who stood between me and the door. That night, however, was the first night the universe would ask me: what are you willing to do to be joyfully free *and* happy, and to heal from the life you have lived? Jump out a window?

After more than three decades of doing healing work in communities impacted by different types of violence, I know and understand that most people do not respond the way I did and do. How I chose to cope as a child is one response to trauma. Even at the age of six something in me resisted lying down and opening my legs when told to do so. I still cannot speak or write publicly about what I did to protect myself. That would expose me to another type of violence from those who would try to shame me for taking control of my own life. At age six. The stories I told myself were shields that protected me by offering a counter word, action, sound, and narrative to everything I was told and everything that was done to me. As a young adult, something in me resisted other people's fears and concerns about telling my business. My "mad woman" has always been with me because she had been awakened very early in me. And, she insisted that I take radical action if it was the only way to save myself.

Freshman year. One night. A living room in a yellow-brick building on Central Street. A Midwestern town. I knew what would happen if I did not respond to the universe with these words, followed by direct action: *Yes! I want to be free. I want to be happy. I want to heal.* It would be easy and "neat" to write that the moment between the couch and the door, when I needed to decide if to jump out the window or knock down the man before me, that this moment was the defining one that shaped my response—despite the fact that I was terrified two men would rape me. It was not. Instead, the long history of sexual violence against me as a child and my refusal to be silent and invisible made it possible to stand up and yell "I want to go home! Now!" Those six words were my "NO!"[11] I still remember shaking inside, holding myself so tightly so I would not fall apart, but also so that my body would be tight and impenetrable, and hard and fast like a bullet. After that evening, I vowed never to give back what I had protected. I vowed never to reconsider if my decision to "own myself fully" was the right one, even when it led to disagreements or accusations of selfishness. More than anything, I vowed to always fight to save my life.

This is not the end of my story, but I will end here.

---

11. This essay has given me an opportunity to see connections in my past and present lives that I had not seen before.

This is my story. My story defines me. I want to remember this story. It is my responsibility: the story and the telling of the story. I tell the story to be free. I tell the story to help others get free. I tell the story so that we can all stay free.

Ase-o!

REFERENCES

Clark Hine, Darlene. "Rape and the Inner Lives of Black Women in the Middle West. *Signs*, vol. 14, no. 4, 1989, pp. 912–920. *Common Grounds and Crossroads: Race, Ethnicity, and Class in Women's Lives*, www.jstor.org/stable/3174692.

Hamilton, Maria. *What Is Now Unaswerable*. Evanston, Illinois: Warrior Poets Press, 1994.

Hartman, Saidiya V. Scenes of Subjection: Terror, Slavery, and Self-Making in Nineteenth-Century America. New York: Oxford University Press, 1997.

McGuire, Danielle L. "It Was like All of Us Had Been Raped': Sexual Violence, Community Mobilization, and the African American Freedom Struggle." *The Journal of American History*, vol. 91, no. 3, Dec. 20014, pp. 906–931.

Scarry, Elaine. *The Body in Pain: The Making and Unmaking of the World*. New York: Oxford University Press, 1987.

Simmons, Aishah Shahidah. *Love with Accountability: Digging up the Roots of Child Sexual Abuse*. Chico, CA: AK Press, 2020.

Van der Kolk, Bessel. *The Body Keeps the Score: Brain, Mind, and Body in the Healing of Trauma*. Penguin Books, 2014. pp 203-204.

PART FIVE

PERSEPHONE

ZILIA BALKANSKY-SELLÉS

Hades was a suitable husband,
we could argue,
even though his courtship and rape of Persephone
was questionable.
Ruler of one third of the universe.
Brother to Zeus.
Lord of the underworld.
Ruler, truly, of any mortal for longer
than Zeus high above.

A hard-struck bargain
compels Persephone's return
each year, and Demeter's sorrow
to be assuaged with the months
of fruitful return, each departure withering
the Earth while her daughter is away;
the fallow sorrow of separation
and loss, undergirding each new spring.

And now, as Australia burns,
and ice sheets fall, island-sized,
into warming seas,

as hungry developers
ward off their fear of death
by ravaging the Earth for
the false security of wealth,
strip-mining mountains,
pouring sludge into toxic rivers and
carving through charred landscapes,
where clear streams once birthed
tadpoles and generations of minnows,
flowing clean drinking water for humans and the myriad otters,
raccoons, bears, crows visiting for sips and swims,
as oceans fill with plastic
driven by the fear of what is finite,
Persephone waits for her release
from the underworld, in a longer winter of despair,
as the frightened avoiders and insurgents of death
and ravaging wealth decimate the Earth.

Let Persephone return;
Let her mother rejoice,
Demeter urging the Earth to bloom,
to restore to wholeness,
to awaken new life.
Let Persephone return
while the fearful scavengers and disrupters make their peace
and quit their frantic avoidances,
celebrating both Demeter and Hades,
the fruitful return and the inevitability
of death that girds all new life.

AUTHOR BIOS

ANTONIA MATTHEW has been writing and doing workshops for the past 10 years. She has given readings at the Writers Guild of Bloomington Poetry and Prose series. Her play, *Homefront,* was performed by readers from the Writers Guild, and friends, and is currently being considered for a radio play, produced locally, using readers from UK's BBC.

BRONISLAVA VOLKOVÁ is a bilingual poet, semiotician, translator, collagist, essayist and Professor Emerita of Indiana University, Bloomington, USA. She is an author of thirty books of poetry, semiotic studies as well as essays and translations. Her work has been translated into a dozen of languages. She currently works and lives in Prague, Czech Republic. More at www.bronislavavolkova.com.

CARA HOHLT eventually found that placing rocks in a garden is more enjoyable than placing words on a page. With this final story, she thanks Tom and Reuben for their valuable feedback. And to David—You take everything that I am, throw it out the window, and it turns into a kite.

CAROLYN GEDULD is the author of two novels, *Take Me Out The Back* (08/2020) and *Who Shall Live* (10/2021), both published by Black Rose Writing in the United States. More than thirty of her short stories have appeared in anthologies and journals such as *Consequence, Steam Ticket Journal, The Writing Disorder,* and *Persimmon Tree.*

DARLENE E. JOLLEY is happily pursuing freedom in multiple ways. She delights in defining "work" as "energy moved." Be present to what is. Alive in the Now. Be gratified. Aim to be kind. Aim to be generous. Recognize each thought as a breath and each breath as a gift from the universe. Thank you for the UNITY. Peace and gratitude.

HÍLDA DAVIS is a writer, educator, and genealogist from Staten Island, New York. Her work has appeared in *The Offing, Callaloo, The Seventh Wave,* and elsewhere. A graduate of the University at Albany and Indiana University–Bloomington, Hílda earned her Master of Fine Arts in Creative Writing from New York University.

HIROMI YOSHIDA is a Pushcart Prize nominee who has authored three poetry chapbooks, *Icarus Burning, Epicanthus,* and *Icarus Redux.* A finalist for the 2019 New Women's Voices Chapbook Competition for *Icarus Burning,* she is also the diversity consultant for the Writers Guild at Bloomington, and a poetry reader for *Flying Island Journal* and *Plath Profiles.*

JAMES DORR'S *The Tears of Isis* was a 2013 Bram Stoker Award® finalist for Fiction Collection, with his latest, *Tombs: A Chronicle of Latter-Day Times of Earth,* a novel-in-stories from Elder Signs Press. He works mostly in horror/dark fantasy with some forays into mystery and SF, and currently harbors a Goth cat named Triana.

JANET CHEATHAM licensed the rights of her self-published quotation collections to Warner Books who published *Famous Black Quotations* in 1995. It is currently being updated. Her memoir, *The Time and Place That Gave Me Life* was published by Indiana University Press in 2007. Henry Louis Gates called her his "hero." For more, see janetcheathambell.com.

JOAN HAWKINS is a Professor of the Cinema and Media Studies at Indiana University Bloomington, and has written extensively on horror and the avant-garde. Her creative work includes a collection of memoir pieces, *School and Suicide;* a limited-edition poetry chapbook, *The Burroughs Hour;* and—with Kyle Quass—the CD *Pragis.*

KALYNN HUFFMAN BROWER can be found growing an edible forest while writing SolarPunk novels and screenplays. Under the pen name K. H. Brower, she imagines a flourishing future in her Bosque Family Adventure Series. Her fictional heros are teenagers on a mission to restore ecosystems across the galaxy, and at the same time reconnect their heart-centered family. www.khbrower.com.

MARIA E. HAMILTON ABEGUNDE, PH.D., is a Memory Keeper. Her works use contemplative practices and ritual to explore bodies as sites of memory, with the understanding that memory never dies, is subversive, and can be recovered to transform and heal transgenerational trauma. She is a professor of African American and African Diaspora Studies at Indiana University Bloomington.

RUTH NOVACZEK (London, UK) is an artist, filmmaker, performance artist, musician and writer; she has exhibited her experimental, vernacular films and installations nationally and internationally since the 1990s. Her films portray a restless, nomadic autofictional landscape, and an eccentric romantic queer feminism. The fragmented narrative in her films is echoed in her prose and poems. On the margins of academia, teaching as a visiting artist, she has a PhD by practice from the University of Westminster where she's a visiting research fellow and is on the faculty of the lo-res Transart Institute (in Berlin). Her work has been shown at galleries and venues including Queer Thoughts, New York, Berlin Arsenal, LUX London, the Kunsthalle New York, Tate Britain, Stuttgart Kunsthalle, Toyota Museum Japan, and in numerous film festivals including Viper Switzerland, Mix NYC, the London Film Festival and Oberhausen, Germany. ruthnovaczek.com.

SHANA RITTER'S poetry and short stories have appeared in various journals and magazines including *Lilith*, *Fifth Wednesday*, and *Georgetown Review*. Her chapbook, *Stairs of Separation*, was published by Finishing Line Press. *In the Time of Leaving*, a novel of exile and resilience set in late-fifteenth-century Spain, was published in 2019. A Pushcart Prize nominee, she has been awarded the Indiana Individual Artist Grant on multiple occasions.

TOM BITTERS has been a Bloomington resident and a Writer's Guild member since 2013. He is retired and volunteers at the Monroe County Public Library, leading conversation groups and tutoring ESL learners. His short fiction has appeared in *Hampshire Life, Peninsular,* and *Meat for Tea.*

ANTONIA MATTHEW has been writing and doing workshops for the past ten years. She has given readings at the Writers Guild of Bloomington Poetry and Prose series. Her play *Homefront* was performed by readers from the Writers Guild, and friends, and is currently being considered for a radio play, produced locally, using readers from UK's BBC.

ZILIA BALKANSKY-SELLÉS was published in *Comparative Woman* (Louisiana State University). The play she co-wrote with Wild Swan Theater, *Myths, Masks, and Magic: World Stories of First Times,* was performed in Michigan schools and libraries and at the University of Michigan Museum of Art. She has given readings at the Writers Guild at Bloomington spoken word events.

ANYA PETERSON ROYCE (photography) Chancellor's Professor of Anthropology Emerita, Indiana University, and Adjunct Professor, University of Limerick, is an ethnographer, drawn especially by its focus on how people can craft satisfying lives for themselves through passion, tenacity, and imagination. She has worked with the Isthmus Zapotec people in Oaxaca, writing about them in Spanish and English, and curating three exhibits of her photographs in Juchitán and at Indiana University. In 2018, The Arts and Culture channel of Mexico (Canal 22) used her photos in a series of documentaries about Juchitán. Her research has also taken her to Poland, Italy, and Ireland looking at identities past and present. In all of this, photography has been essential.

PHOTOGRAPHY BY
Anya Royce Peterson, PhD